SHORT GAME [SECRETS] OF THE PROS

Also by Jay Morelli

Beginning Golf

The Original Golf School Way

Age Is Not a Handicap

SHORT GAME [SECRETS] OF THE PROS

Club Pros from Around the World
Reveal Their Secrets to Better Golf

JAY MORELLI

New York   Chicago   San Francisco   Lisbon   London   Madrid   Mexico City
Milan   New Delhi   San Juan   Seoul   Singapore   Sydney   Toronto

Library of Congress Cataloging-in-Publication Data

Morelli, Jay.
    Short game secrets of the pros : club pros from around the world reveal their secrets to
better golf / Jay Morelli ; with Photographs by Bruce Curtis.
       p.   cm.
    Includes index.
    ISBN 0-07-146981-8 (alk. paper)
    1. Short game (Golf).   I. Title.

GV979.S54S636   2007
796.352'3—dc22   2006027390

1 2 3 4 5 6 7 8 9 10 11 12 13 14 15 16 17 18 19 20 21 22 23 DOC/DOC 0 9 8 7

ISBN-13: 978-0-07-146981-4
ISBN-10:   0-07-146981-8

Interior design by Think Design

Photographs by Bruce Curtis

McGraw-Hill books are available at special quantity discounts to use as premiums and sales
promotions, or for use in corporate training programs. For more information, please write to the
Director of Special Sales, Professional Publishing, McGraw-Hill, Two Penn Plaza, New York, NY
10121-2298. Or contact your local bookstore.

This book is printed on acid-free paper.

I would like to dedicate this book to my wonderful family

and especially to my recently deceased parents,

"Moe" and John Morelli.

Contents

Foreword

Jay and I have been golf professionals and friends for an awfully long time. We've seen a lot of tips and instruction come and go. What with the Golf Channel, instructional segments during golf telecasts, and tips in various golf magazines, we have been bombarded with information on how to play this wonderful game.

All of this information can be overwhelming and confusing. What Jay has tried to accomplish in this book is to draw on the best teachers in the business, to present the practical side of instruction. What are the best teachers saying to their students, and how do they communicate that information? If you're fortunate enough to have a lesson with a top instructor, what will be his or her approach?

This book is a compilation of that information. For the newer player, it is a total foundation for the short game. For the experienced player, it may contain that secret or two that will prove a key to curing short game woes that have been with you forever. If you want to become an instructor, this book will provide a good cross-section of what the best in the business say and believe.

This is not a cookie-cutter approach to instruction. You will read several different ways to approach the short game. Try some of these styles to see which one suits you best. We are all athletes, and there are different horses for different courses. The bottom line is that this book will provide you with the tools to lower your score. It will be a big help, regardless of your level, and take strokes off your game. I know Jay will enjoy that.

Dave Pfannenstein
Director of Golf, Killington Golf Course

Acknowledgments

My sincerest thanks to the professional instructors who took time from their busy schedules to help me with this book.

And another thank-you to all of the teaching professionals around the country who have helped thousands of golfers better enjoy their game. This book is really about us, the teaching professionals.

A special thanks to Ann Giacomozzi who helped me organize the text. And to Lisa Stracks for her work in copyediting the manuscript.

Thanks also to my partner, Bruce Curtis, for the great photography.

Introduction

What is it that can be so confounding about the short shots—putting, chipping, and pitching? We all know the joy of really crushing a tee shot. Over time, though, we realize that those big tee shots have very little to do with how we score and that the short game is the key to scoring.

The first step to success in the short game is having the ability to picture the best possible shot for the situation. You have to be able to visualize what you are trying to do if you have a chance to do it.

The second step is to understand how to hit that short shot correctly. Where do you play the ball in your stance? How much swing do you use? Do you have the correct grip? The answers to these and other questions will help improve your short game.

To showcase a good spectrum of teaching methods, I thought it would be a good idea to ask the best teachers at the finest courses how they taught their students. The professionals who contributed to this book are a very special group. They have won countless awards. Two of these professionals, Ken Morton Sr. and Jim Brotherton have received the PGA's highest honor: The PGA Professional of the Year. All have won regional and statewide recognition for their teaching accomplishments. Most of all, they have collectively helped thousands of golfers improve their golf games. Try their suggestions, and see how they work for you.

The third step is practice. Once you have figured out some fundamentals, the short shots require finesse and feel. You can only achieve that by doing. Once you get the correct feel around the green, you will get better results. Improved results lead to increased confidence, and confidence feeds on itself. By using visualization, good concepts, and practice, your short game will keep improving and your scores will keep going down.

The Short Game

All golfers want to improve their scores. The serious golfers, of course, and even the non-serious golfers, who say that golf is just a good walk in the park and just good exercise, want to improve their scores. It's the nature of the game. The score is how we measure our performance and improvement.

The majority of strokes for all players are within 50 yards of the green. That statistic holds true for the entire golf world, whether the player is a PGA or LPGA Tour player or just a weekend golfer. The best way to lower that score, therefore, is to improve the short game. It's as simple as that.

There seems to be an infinite amount of instruction on how to get that little white ball into the hole. There are so many methods and systems. Which golf guru do you listen to, and which one is the best for you? What methods do the best teachers use? Have they had great success in a teaching technique that is unconventional? The answer is to examine the available instruction and see which system suits you best.

The teachers interviewed in this book are not the gurus that you see working with Tiger Woods or Phil Mickelson (although many of them do teach PGA and LPGA touring professionals and also started many of those stars in junior clinics at their course). Rather, they are the teachers who seek to improve the score of the average golfer. They have learned their craft by teaching countless hours with hundreds or thousands of golfers. They have sorted through the challenges facing everyday golfers on how to improve around the greens. These teachers have developed valid systems and have achieved positive results.

Golfers are athletes, not robots, and you must be comfortable with a style if you are going to develop confidence. All great teachers agree that confidence is a key ingredient to better technique and, thus, lower scores. Confidence is a product of finesse and knowledge.

The short game requires very little strength. Even a small child can hit the ball far enough for the short game. To improve takes finesse and technique. Finesse, or feel, is that ability that we have to control the distance and direction that we hit the ball. We all have been born with different amounts of finesse, just as we all were born with different aptitude for music or art.

Technique is a product of learning, it is knowledge, it is know-how. The great Canadian player and teacher, George Knudson, said it best: "It is difficult in life to do something if you don't understand what you're trying to do." When you are learning something, you should have a clear picture of what to do and how to do it. So, in this book, I have compiled some basic techniques that are taught daily. All of the teaching styles contained in this book are not alike—they couldn't be. But you will see many common fundamentals among the methods these fine teachers use. These common fundamentals are mentioned often because they have worked over time. They should be the basis for most of your strokes around the green. You will also read some different and unconventional approaches; while these may not fit you, they may help you with a particular aspect of your short game. As I mentioned before, we are not robots, and a new way of getting the ball in the hole may be just what the doctor ordered.

Tom Nieporte

Head Professional Emeritus, Winged Foot Golf Club

The Short Game

In reflecting on his career as both a player and a teacher, Tom feels that not enough emphasis has been placed on learning the short game. He estimates that out of the many thousands of lessons he has given over fifty years of teaching, he has probably given less than twenty-five putting lessons.

Looking back, he wishes that he had motivated his students to take more putting lessons, because it's the only place to make a dramatic impact on the score. To illustrate, Tom says that even Tiger Woods and Jack Nicklaus, at their best, could only save four strokes to par by having an immaculate long game, and that is if they hit all four par 5s on the typical course in two rather than three strokes, saving four strokes to regulation. But if they have a brilliant putting

Tom Nieporte is the head professional emeritus at Winged Foot Golf Club in Mamaroneck, New York. He has been one of the premier players in the Ohio and Metropolitan sections of the PGA, and he is the last true club professional to have won a PGA Tour event, the Bob Hope Desert Classic in 1967.

Winged Foot Golf Club is arguably one of the finest golf courses in the country. It has hosted, at one time or another, almost all of the major USGA competitions as well as the PGA Championship.

round and only use twenty-five or twenty-six putts (which they fairly often do), they can save ten or eleven strokes to par.

> He likens the putting stroke to the pendulum on a grandfather clock: the pendulum swings back, sets, and then changes direction. There is no rush to change direction in the clock's pendulum, and there should be no rush in the putting stroke to change direction.

Putting

When it comes to the mechanics of putting, Tom feels that Ben Crenshaw changed the golf world by developing a putting stroke that was more of a pendulum arm-and-shoulder stroke than a wrist or hitting action, which had been used for so long on the typically slower greens of earlier years. The Crenshaw putting style was quickly adapted by his fellow competitors when they saw how successful it was for Gentle Ben.

Today Tom teaches that style to his students. It's a no-wrist, even stroke; there is no hitting action, just a smooth stroke using arms and shoulders. He likens the putting stroke to the pendulum on a grandfather clock: the pendulum swings back, sets, and then changes direction. There is no rush to change direction in the clock's pendulum, and there should be no rush in the putting stroke to change direction. He says that good putters let the putter "set" at the end of the backstroke, just like the pendulum on the grandfather clock.

Tom notes that there are alternative methods of putting, such as putting cross-handed, using the long putter, or even just making subtle changes in your putting grip. If you are having trouble, he suggests that you experiment to find a style that is more comfortable for you. He has seen some of the great players change their styles to save their careers, such as

Sam Snead, who putted side-saddle later in his career, and Bruce Lietzke, a current Senior PGA Tour player, who now uses the long putter.

Chipping

Tom teaches that you should visualize the easiest possible chip shot, one that lands on the green and then rolls to the flagstick. If you have plenty of green between you and the flagstick, he recommends using a 4 or a 5 iron and a short swing. He then says to turn the toe of the chipping club slightly inward and, with a short backswing, "drag" the ball toward the hole. The slightly closed face and the feeling of dragging the ball will produce a low running chip that will stay very low, almost hugging the ground as the ball travels to the hole. To help get the feeling for how fast and how hard to hit the ball, Tom uses the analogy of pitching pennies underhand. It's a similar action, a backswing, a forward swing, and a follow-through. Other principles he passes on are: first, to keep your head still, as unnecessary motion on a short shot will only complicate a simple movement, and second, to focus on a dimple on the golf ball, as short shots are often mishit because the player looked up before the ball was hit, resulting in poor contact and a poor result.

To play this stroke, Tom suggests that you shorten up on the handle, put your feet together, and use a short swing. Importantly, he notes that the clubface angle should never change, neither opening nor closing as it would in the normal full swing. This action is a pendulum-type swing with no wrist action.

To help get the feeling for how fast and how hard to hit the ball, Tom uses the analogy of pitching pennies underhand. It's a similar action, a backswing, a forward swing, and a follow-through.

Tom emphasizes that you have to discover a system with which you are comfortable, as there are different strokes for different folks. He mentions Roberto DiVencenzo, a great professional from Argentina, who was winner of the British Open and of every major title in South America as well as runner-up in the Masters. Roberto used only a sand wedge around the green and was a true master with that club. A member at Winged Foot, Hank Malfa, has also impressed Tom with his use of the sand wedge around the green, supporting the point that golfers can be taught the fundamentals but that many individual preferences come with the game. Tom stresses that you shouldn't be afraid to try a different approach if you're having trouble in a certain aspect of the short game.

Imagination

Tom feels that you do have some ability to picture a shot that you are going to hit. And he recommends keeping your eyes open for new ways to play a shot. By way of illustration, he recounts a great story about imagination. He was playing with Gene Borek in the Metropolitan PGA at Winged Foot. On the 16th hole, Gene hit the ball dead behind a tree. The tree was too tall to hit a ball over and the branches were too low for Gene to slide a shot under the tree. Beyond the tree, it was downhill to the hole. It was a distance of about 30 yards. Gene tried a most imaginative shot. He pitched the ball into the tree, about two thirds of the way up the tree. The ball bounced down through the branches, much like a pinball in a pinball machine. The ball finally landed on the downhill slope just short of the green and kept rolling until it nestled up by the pin. Now that's imagination!

Jim Cocchi

Director of Golf and General Manager,
Seville Golf Club

Putting

Jim is an advocate of the long putter. He finds that it is particularly helpful for golfers who have putted well in the past and then completely lost their touch, something he sees happen to a lot of players. He feels that the ball rolls better with the long putter than the standard shorter putter. What Jim likes about this approach is that it reduces anxiety, which automatically creates confidence. Since he has adopted this approach, he has never stood over a putt with doubt that he would make it. In Jim's words, "putting with the long putter is like stealin', it's just too easy."

To use the long putter successfully, Jim recommends that it fit so that the end of the club rests snugly on your chest. That end of the putter then stays in the same position all

Jim Cocchi is Director of Golf and General Manager of Seville Golf Club in Brooksville, Florida. Jim has been Mr. Golf on the West Coast of Florida, and he received the Teacher of the Year Award from the North Florida Chapter of the PGA. Jim was the driving force in establishing the Suncoast Junior Golf Association, for which he received the PGA Award for Junior Golf in the North Florida Section of the PGA.

Seville Golf Club was designed by noted golf architect Arthur Hill.

through the putting stroke, acting as an anchor from which the club swings. According to Jim, the benefit of this style of putting is that there are fewer moving parts. Your top hand holds the putter close to the chest, while your bottom hand freely swings the putter. Jim likens this approach to that of a pool player who stabilizes the cue with the front hand and uses the rear hand to generate the power and necessary feel and finesse.

While the long-putter method may only be for a few, Jim applies the same general principle when he teaches the conventional putting method. He says that the left shoulder is the pivot point for the putting stroke and that for consistent results you should rotate your shoulders. Your left shoulder starts first, and then the movement of your shoulders swings the putter. He recommends reducing hand action as much as possible so that your shoulders swing the putter head.

When teaching the putting stroke, Jim recommends that you practice putt with either hand—first putting a few balls with your right hand, then a few with your left. Invariably, you will find that one hand has more control of distance and direction and feels better. Jim says that the hand that has the best "feel" is the hand that should dominate the putting stroke: if your right hand is more dominant, concentrate on a right-hand stroke; if your left hand appears more dominant, concentrate on a left-hand stroke.

Jim suggests alternative styles if you aren't feeling confident. He recommends the cross-handed grip or, for right-handed players, a left-hand low grip. These styles help you rely on the use of your shoulders and not your hands in the putting stroke. Another alternative style Jim suggests is the Bernhard Langer style, where your right hand holds on to your left forearm (this is certainly an alternative style and looks funny, but it sure works for Bernhard).

Jim notes that learning how hard to stroke the ball on the green for a putt takes practice. He also believes that distance control should be consistent—you shouldn't try to ease in a putt on one hole and then be very aggressive on the next hole. He feels that putting the ball the correct distance is certainly one of the keys to being a better putter, and it's a skill that comes easier to some than others. Learning distance control is the product of experience and visualization, he says. Experience comes from hours on the putting green and having a lot of golf under your belt. Visualization comes from taking the time to picture what the ball will look like rolling toward the hole.

Ultimately, Jim feels that putting is an art, not a science, and requires both feel and imagination. He states, "Putting is art. If it was a science, all golfers would putt the same way."

> Visualization comes from taking the time to picture what the ball will look like rolling toward the hole.

Chipping

According to Jim, the chipping stroke should be similar to the putting stroke. The clubhead should swing low to the ground. Jim's goal is to get the ball on the green as quickly as possible—in other words, to have the ball land on the green and then roll like a putt. He doesn't believe in carrying the ball too far on to the green. Jim uses what he calls the "dead ball" approach—a putting-style stroke that ensures that the ball doesn't spin too much. Because the ball has no or little spin, it will roll more consistently. A ball hit with a lot of spin may "grab" on the green, making it more difficult to control the distance.

An interesting change Jim has made in his own game is to use the ten-finger grip when chipping. In the ten-finger grip, both hands hold the handle of the club, with no interlocking or overlapping of the fingers. This approach has given Jim and some of his students a lot more feel. It also may create a little less spin so that the ball will roll more like a putt.

Pitching

To hit the pitch shot, Jim thinks that you should use the pitching or gap wedge, as these clubs were designed for this shot. He is not a big believer in the 60-degree wedges for most golfers. He feels that you have to hit them too hard, that you seldom reach the hole, and that the mishits are too costly.

He also teaches that you vary the distance you hit by varying the size of the swing, which you learn by "feel" and practice. One slight difference in Jim's approach from usual techniques is to have the clubface a little "open" at address (so that the face of the club points slightly to the right of the target for right-handed players). Jim says, "I've never seen anyone really pitch the ball well with the clubface even slightly closed."

Jim has a simple rule that all golfers should follow: when you leave the cart to play a ball that is off the green, take three clubs with you: the putter, the 7 iron, and a wedge. Your first choice of club is the putter. If, however, you feel that there is too much grass to putt through, then use the 7 iron. And if you feel that the 7 iron won't provide enough loft, use the wedge. From his perspective, the putter is the simplest and most reliable club to use, the 7 iron still

> Jim has a simple rule that all golfers should follow: when you leave the cart to play a ball that is off the green, take three clubs with you: the putter, the 7 iron, and a wedge.

makes for a fairly easy shot, and the wedge is a more difficult club and should be used only when extra loft is required.

Bunker Shots

Jim says that bunker shots are "the easiest shot in the book, because all you do is use the bounce of the wedge [the added metal on the bottom of the club] to slide the club through the sand and move a divot of sand out of the bunker and on to the green." He also has another variation on a theme for bunker play. He suggests that when you have a long bunker shot (probably the most difficult shot in the game), you use a club other than a sand wedge. For long bunker shots, Jim suggests that you use the standard method of hitting a bunker shot, but use a pitching or gap wedge. He also says that if you get fairly comfortable, you can even try the long bunker shots with an 8 or a 9 iron. This does require some practice, he acknowledges, but it is the best way to turn one of the hardest strokes in the game into a "not-so-hard" shot.

Confidence

The key to an improved short game is confidence, and Jim feels that the trick is to reduce and eliminate anxiety. You have to be certain of what you're trying to do and not second-guess your plan. Take the time to make a good plan, commit to it, and proceed.

Jim feels that another way to reduce anxiety is to have a good preshot routine. A preshot routine consists of the motions you make before you play the stroke, and any routine you create is better than not having one at all. He asks, for example, do you look at the target two or three times? Do you practice the swing before the actual swing? Think about what you usually do and develop your own consistent routine.

Jim's suggestion for a good routine is:

1. Take a short practice swing.
2. Set the clubhead behind the ball.
3. Set your feet and take the stance.
4. Look at the target two or three times.
5. Swing away.

Jim emphasizes that the most important feature of a good preshot routine is that it is consistent in manner and in time.

Joan McDonald

Head Professional, Gleneagles Golf Course

Putting

Joan's first concern regarding putting is determining the length of the club. She feels that most golfers putt with a putter that is too long. Her recommendation is that the putter be short enough to let your arms stretch out when you address the ball. If your arms are able to hang from your shoulders in a relaxed, extended position, more of a pendulum motion will be made, thus eliminating unnecessary hand or wrist action. In the photo sequence on the following page, notice how Joan's arms are relaxed and there is no wrist break.

On short putts (3 feet or less), Joan's tip is to shorten up on the handle, even down to the shaft; place your feet closer together than you would on your longer putts; and concentrate on the rhythm of your stroke. She notes that

Joan McDonald is the head professional at the Gleneagles Golf Course at the Equinox Resort in Manchester, Vermont. Prior to accepting the position at the Equinox, Joan was the head professional at Morefar Golf Club in Brewster, New York, and the teaching professional at Winged Foot Golf Club in Mamaroneck, New York, during the summers and Indian Creek Country Club in Bal Harbor, Florida, and Black Diamond Ranch in Lecanto, Florida, during the winters. Joan has qualified for three U.S. Opens and has won the Maryland Women's Open.

The Equinox was designed in 1927 by Walter Travis, one of the finest players and course architects of his era.

A good putting stroke is like the pendulum on a grandfather clock. Your arms and shoulders smoothly swing the putter away from and then toward the hole.

most putts that are missed from this distance are missed because they were rushed. She focuses instead on a slow and even stroke, defining an even stroke as the same pace back and through. Her philosophy is that you don't need distance here and therefore you don't need speed, so keep it slow and rhythmical. This is especially true on fast greens.

On short putts, Joan also suggests that you take the "break" out by putting firmly, into the back of the hole. She advocates concentrating on finishing your follow-through—keep your head steady and don't let it come up until after the putt is well on its way.

Chipping

Joan teaches that setup is the key to making chip shots. Most missed chips are due to a poor setup position. She insists that you take sufficient time and make a mental checklist of the different steps. First, identify the lie, the distance to the hole, and slope of the green. She asks, are you going uphill, side-hill, downhill? Is the ball in the rough or fairway? All of these factors will determine club selection. Second, she recommends that you play the ball back in the stance. Joan feels that most players don't position the ball far enough back in the stance. Your hands should be positioned more off the front thigh than centered, and your weight should be positioned more toward the front foot. Third, Joan says that the rhythm of the chipping stroke should be smooth, backward and forward. Allow yourself time to finish the backswing motion before you start swinging down and through. Finally, Joan says that swinging the club with shoulders and arms rather than wrists and hands will help you hit the ball more on the downswing.

Pitching

Joan says that the only way to really get good at pitch shots is to practice—there is no alternative. She thinks that the pitch shot requires much confidence and to get that confidence you must rehearse. You need to feel where the clubhead is and control the length of your swing. She maintains that it is important to feel the club set (the correct wrist hinge) on the backswing and to allow your wrists to hinge even though it is a short swing. The correct hinge will help you hit the ball on the downswing and keep you from scooping the ball, which is usually what happens when you mishit a pitch shot.

She notes that most putts that are missed from this distance are missed because they were rushed. She focuses instead on a slow and even stroke, defining an even stroke as the same pace back and through.

As with the chip shot, Joan thinks that the setup is a key element in the pitch shot. She teaches that the stance should be a little more narrow than a regular full shot. She also says that it is really important to keep the lower body from moving too much and recommends trying to eliminate any side-to-side motion with the hips or up-and-down motion with the legs. Although your weight moves back and through, you should try to keep your lower body a little more steady.

Bunker Shots

Joan says, "If you're ever going to be a good player out of a bunker, you must think you're a good bunker player!" For starters, she has her students visualize the shot before they stand over the ball and picture what they want to do.

Most successful sand shots require a high lofted shot. To achieve this, Joan states that you'll need to make a fairly long backswing and thorough follow-through. She teaches that you finish the swing with your weight on your front foot. Mentally, this can be difficult to do because you're so close to the green, but she maintains that it's important to commit to a full follow-through to generate the speed to move the ball and the sand out of the bunker.

According to Joan, there are three steps to good bunker play. First, make sure that your weight is evenly distributed or even slightly favors the front foot. Second, your stance should be slightly opened and the ball positioned forward. Third and most important, try to keep your arms tension-free and your grip pressure very soft. This will allow you to feel the clubhead in your swing and also help the club "splash" the sand. If your grip pressure and arms are tight, she says, you will pull up out of the shot, the clubhead will miss the sand, and you'll hit the ball too clean.

Handling Pressure

Joan feels that the short game is more affected by jitters than the long game because the motions required for putting, chipping, pitching, and bunker shots are smooth and soft. When we become nervous, we tend to rush the shot and rely on our hands rather than on the swinging action of the club. She suggests that you concentrate on using your shoulders to start your motion and to keep a good rhythm.

Joan also recommends getting in a good routine before each shot to give yourself time to run through a checklist of key elements for that particular situation. Most mistakes occur in both the long game and the short game because of something in the setup, which in turn creates a lack of confidence. Joan suggests that students learn a good preshot routine with a mental checklist for the setup and visualize positive swings and results. These keys will help you become more consistent under pressure.

Joan also recommends getting in a good routine before each shot to give yourself time to run through a checklist of key elements for that particular situation.

Jim Morris

Head Professional, National Golf Links of America

Putting

When Jim begins working on putting, he will first have you putt with either hand individually so that he can figure out which hand has the most "feel." Once that has been determined, he builds the stroke around that dominant hand. He will also have you putt with that one hand as a practice drill to achieve feel and distance control and accelerate the putter toward the hole using that dominant hand. He says that you should not be overly conscious of the ball during the stroke but focus on the hole. Swing the putter head toward the hole and let the ball just get in the way of the stroke. The focus should be on the line and the hole, not on the ball.

Jim has had good success teaching putting with some different and unconventional styles.

Jim Morris is the head professional at the National Golf Links of America located in Southampton, on the eastern end of Long Island, New York. Before that, Jim was the teaching professional at Deepdale Golf Club in Manhasset, New York, for three years and the head professional at Frenchman's Creek in Palm Beach Gardens, Florida, for five years. He has been rated by *Golf Digest* as one of the best teachers in New York and ranked in the top 100 in the Northeast by *Golf Magazine*.

The National was built in 1904 and has been consistently ranked one of the *Golf Digest* Top 100 courses in America. It is a true links-style course.

He notes that the long putter is always a good method to try when the standard club isn't working for you. He has also had particularly good luck with the claw putting grip. The claw is a grip that has helped many PGA tour players, including Chris DeMarco, who says that it saved his career.

To change to the claw grip, Jim suggests that you hold the putter in the top hand as you normally would, then place your bottom hand on the handle so that the handle rests between your thumb and middle finger. The four fingers of your bottom hand will rest on the top of the handle. You will be able to see all four knuckles of your bottom hand, and it will look more like a claw than a hand. The concept is to neutralize the effect the bottom hand has on the swinging action of the putter. It makes the stroke feel more like a shoulder action than a hand action, which produces a smoother, more reliable putting stroke. "Ray Floyd told me that there are four keys to great putting: comfort, style, speed, and confidence," Jim says. "The style that feels best is the right one for you. Putting is like a restaurant menu—not everyone has the same taste."

Jim teaches that you should putt the ball with enough speed to comfortably pass the hole. The speed dictates the line, for a ball putted with sufficient speed will obviously "break" less than a putt that does not reach the hole. Jim says, "I have found that PGA Tour professionals dive the ball into the hole, they seldom just reach the hole and fall in."

For advanced players, Jim likes to focus on the path and angle of the blade of the putter. He asks, is the blade square to the line? Is the putter being swung straight back and straight through to the hole? If you are one of these advanced players, Jim will have you putt with only your dominant hand from 10 feet away from the hole. If done properly, the putter will feel light and swing freely, and the ball will roll true.

> Swing the putter head toward the hole and let the ball just get in the way of the stroke. The focus should be on the line and the hole, not on the ball.

Chipping and Pitching

Jim feels that chipping and pitching are dictated by setup. For the standard chip or pitch, he recommends positioning the ball about center in the stance. To hit the shot a little lower or if the ball is on hard ground, position the ball a little toward your rear foot. If the ball is sitting up in the grass or you want a little higher trajectory, position the ball more forward in the stance.

Jim says that you should concentrate on using your forearms when you hit these short shots rather than making a pure shoulder movement. He finds that using the shoulders too much on this shot creates too big a swing and some rocking motion. The rocking motion tends to have the player hit the ball too much on the upswing, causing topped or thin shots that run through the green. He prefers using the forearms and focusing on two things: the location desired for landing the ball and the rotation of the forearms, which creates a shallow angle that will ensure better contact.

A drill that Jim finds always helps keep the body and legs quiet is to hit some practice shots with your legs crossed. This helps you rely on your forearms to swing the club and eliminates any excess movements. This also helps you establish a shallow swing, as the clubhead has a constant arc and the proper angle when it comes to the ball.

As for which club to use for pitching and chipping, Jim is not a big advocate of highly lofted wedges for most golfers. He feels that lob or 60-degree wedges are subject to the skill level of the golfer. Unless you are very advanced or a professional, he encourages you to use the standard 56-degree sand wedge for lofted shots around the green. He finds that there are several advantages to using this club. First, the 56-degree wedge offers plenty of loft for almost any shot. Second, most golfers use it most of the time anyway, so you may as well

> A drill that Jim finds always helps keep the body and legs quiet is to hit some practice shots with your legs crossed.

stick with the one club you're comfortable with rather than switch it around when it really isn't necessary. Third, golfers simply have to swing too hard with a 60-degree wedge to reach the hole. The majority of recreational golfers slice the ball, which means that the clubface is open. An open clubface and a 60-degree wedge will produce a shot that is extremely high and short, a very poor percentage shot. So his advice is to stick with the 56-degree wedge for all lofted shots around the green and leave the lob or 60-degree wedge in the car.

Bunker Shots

When it comes to bunker shots, Jim feels that it is very important to learn how to use the bounce of the wedge. The bounce is the extra metal on the back of the sand wedge that prevents it from digging into the sand and instead allows it to glide through the sand. This action produces a shallow divot of sand. If the ball is anywhere inside the divot, the ball and the divot will come popping out of the sand.

Jim's key to the bunker shot is the pace of the follow-through, which controls the distance the ball will travel. The faster the pace, the farther the ball will go. The slower paced follow-through will produce a lower and shorter ball flight. One of the drills he has had the most success with is having you swing the club in the sand bunker with the right hand only. This drill helps you acquire the feel for the length and pace of the swing. More importantly, it allows you to get the feel for the depth of the splash. He notes that it's almost impossible to successfully do the splash drill with one hand and not take the correct shallow divot. Taking too much sand in the bunker and swinging the club too deeply into the sand will result in the clubhead staying in the sand. The result will be no follow-through and the ball staying in the sand.

Long greenside bunker shots are always difficult, so Jim advises using a pitching wedge. He finds that because the pitching wedge has less loft than the sand wedge, it is much easier to hit the ball farther on this shot and thus reach the flagstick. He also finds that using the pitching wedge makes players more confident that they can reach the hole. This reduces stress and anxiety—a very good thing.

Keeping It Clear and Simple

One of the principles Jim has learned as a teacher is to keep lessons as simple as possible and not tell students everything he knows about a particular technique or stroke. He'd like to pass that idea along to recreational golfers who may have encountered instruction that became confusing. As a student, you're trying to develop a feel for the shot, not to learn everything there is to know about it. If you are overwhelmed by too much information, don't be afraid to ask your instructor to simplify the information. You'll be doing both the instructor and yourself a favor.

In general, in the short game, Jim finds that good results build confidence. As a teacher, Jim believes that to achieve good results and help players gain confidence, the key is to have your instructor properly diagnose your flaws and then clearly communicate the proper correction. Your instructor should then confirm that the plan of correction is clear and that you understand exactly how you're going to effect change. Only then, Jim says, can you and your instructor move together as a team toward game improvement.

6

Tom Joyce

Director of Golf, Glen Oaks Country Club

Putting

Tom's first piece of advice regarding putting is a great tip he received many years ago from one of golf's best putters, George Archer. George said that during the putting stroke, the left shoulder (the right shoulder for left-handers) goes down on the backstroke and up on the forward stroke. Tom notes that many golfers turn their shoulders, a move similar to the regular swing, when they putt, but that moving the front shoulder down on the back-stroke keeps the putter blade square to the hole longer.

When teaching putting, Tom works first on alignment. He says that lining up the putter blade squarely to the hole is essential. If the putter blade is misaligned, the best stroke in the world will putt the ball off line. When

Tom Joyce is a PGA Life Member and was the long-standing Director of Golf at Glen Oaks Country Club in Old Westbury, New York. Tom has won all of the major tournaments in the New York metropolitan area and has twice won the National Senior PGA Club Professional Championship.

Glen Oaks is one of the finest courses in the New York metropolitan area. It was designed by Joseph S. Finger and opened in 1971.

working with you, Tom will stand behind you so that he can check the alignment of the putter and then make the necessary adjustments. (You can do this yourself by having a golfing friend stand behind you when you address and aim the putter. There are also putter training devices that produce a laser light showing where the putter is aimed.) He feels that you have to get used to looking at the adjusted alignment, which is not as easy as it sounds. If you have had the putter blade aimed to the left or right of the target for years, the correction to square the putter blade will seem unbelievable and take plenty of reinforcement. Tom finds that misalignment is an old habit that dies hard.

After fixing the alignment, Tom works on the speed of the putt. The speed will affect how much the ball breaks, so it is essential to practice hard to develop a feel for speed. Tom encourages you to spend plenty of time practicing. He also suggests drills that help develop feel, such as putting from the center of the green toward the edge of the green. Doing this from several angles will give you a good feel for the speed of the greens, particularly if you're playing a new course.

Tom offers a few important rules about putting:

> A rather "off the wall" tip Tom gives good putters who are having a tough time is to putt with their eyes closed.

1. Never leave a putt short, as the putt will definitely not go in the hole.
2. Never decelerate (slow down the speed of the stroke).
3. Realize that "nothing lasts forever"; in other words, a certain feel or concept may not continue to have positive results, in which case it's time to develop a new feel.

Tom feels there are a few traits great putters have: (1) the ability to read greens (determine how much the ball will break) and (2) the ability to control the ball's speed.

A rather "off the wall" tip Tom gives good putters who are having a tough time is to putt with their eyes closed. It's a good way to practice, and it can work on the golf course.

Chipping

Tom teaches that, as much as possible, you should chip the ball exactly the same way as you putt. To accomplish this, he first has you select a club to chip with that doesn't have too much loft. He feels that most chip shots should be played with a middle iron—a 5, 6, or 7. Shorten up on the grip about 2 inches so that the iron is approximately the same length as the putter. The ball position should be in the center of the stance, and then you stroke the chip, exactly as you would the putter. Tom says that this style gets the ball on the green and rolling. He also notes that this style has few moving parts and is very repeatable.

The most reliable way to chip is to choose a middle iron and then use a putting grip and a putting stroke.

Pitching

Tom has some important tips for pitch shots (20 to 60 yards). This is an important distance because you don't use a full swing, yet the swing must be longer than a chipping stroke. The pitch shots of this distance require the characteristics of the full swing: some weight shift, some body rotation, and a follow-through.

- Make sure that there is no lateral motion. Any side-to-side motion will create mishits.
- Do use rotation—this miniswing should have the same rotational motion as the full swing.
- For advanced players, the "release" should feel like it's from the left hand.
- Trust the swing, as the swing, not extra hand action, will get results.

For advanced players, Tom teaches the use of the 60- and even the 64-degree wedges. From his perspective, the advantage of these lofted wedges is that good players can almost hit the ball straight up in the air. The disadvantage, of course, is that you must swing hard to hit the ball a short distance, and mishits then can be disasters.

Bunker Shots

If it's a short shot, it requires a short follow-through; if it's a long shot, then a long follow-through.

Tom maintains that the sand shot is one of the easiest in the book, and he has a few suggestions for improving this shot. First, he teaches that you should learn to use the bounce (the added metal on the bottom of the club) of the sand wedge. To use the bounce, he says, first open the stance at address, so that a line across your toes points to the left of the target at address (for right-handed players). Next, aim the clubface at the target. When the clubface is then aimed at the target, it will be "open." This puts the bounce of the wedge closer to the sand than the leading edge of the club. The bounce helps the clubhead slide through the sand and prevents it from digging. In the photo on the left, notice how Tom splashes the sand out of the bunker, using the bounce of the wedge.

In the sand shot, "splash" the sand out of the bunker.

Notice the full follow-through in the sand shot. The sand wedge enters the sand about 2 inches behind the ball. The sand then acts as a cushion, so a full follow-through is needed to move the sand and the ball out of the bunker.

Tom's second suggestion is to weaken the top hand grip a little. He suggests, for example, that if you are right-handed, you change the grip so that the "V" created by the thumb and forefinger of the left hand is pointing more toward your nose than your right shoulder. He says that the effect of this grip change is to make sure that the clubface stays open during the swing, and an open clubface insures that you get the necessary loft while preventing the club from digging into the sand.

Tom's third tip is that you should gauge the distance of the shot by the length of the follow-through. If it's a short shot, it requires a short follow-through; if it's a long shot, then a long follow-through.

7

Susan Stafford

Director and Owner, Roland Stafford Golf Schools

Putting

Susan says that putting is all about feel after you have learned the elusive mechanics. Here are some of the fundamentals she teaches:

1. There should be no movement from the waist down.
2. Your head should stay down for a count of three after the putt has been stroked.
3. The distance of the backstroke should never be longer than the distance of the follow-through.
4. If you are right-handed, the palm of your right hand should face the line of the putt, and your right arm should

Susan Stafford is the Director and owner of the Roland Stafford Golf Schools, which comprises three locations. Susan is acknowledged as a respected business innovator in the area of golf school management, marketing, and golf education. Her interpretation and extension of her late husband's teaching methods continue to improve the golf swings of hundreds of people annually.

The main location for the Roland Stafford Golf Schools is Windham Country Club in Windham, New York. Windham is a 6,500-yard course that requires straight drives and precision shots on the three devilish par 3s. It is rated as a "must play" by *Golf Digest*.

stretch toward the line of the putt on the follow-through. This is reversed if you are left-handed.

5. If you are right-handed, your left elbow should stay flexed so as not to restrict movement and feel. Again, this is reversed if you are left-handed.

For side-hill putts, Susan teaches that you should pick a spot where you think the ball will break and then try to use the correct speed.

To make those nerve-racking short putts, she suggests that you concentrate on hitting the ball 1 foot past the hole and that you not look up until you hear the ball drop.

> To make those nerve-racking short putts, she suggests that you concentrate on hitting the ball 1 foot past the hole and that you not look up until you hear the ball drop.

Chipping

Susan thinks that chipping is a commitment—while the chip shot appears to be a simple stroke, it is a real stroke saver and requires practice and attention. Susan also feels that clubs are like children—you should know what they do. When working on your chipping, she recommends experimenting with different techniques, such as using your putting grip and your putting stroke.

Susan recommends chipping with a 5 or a 6 iron, saying that this technique is great just off the green if your nerves are a little shaky. She also suggests trying different lofted clubs—the less loft, the more roll, and vice versa. She feels that you should consider all conditions before choosing the best club to chip with. Once you have made your decision about the club, you need to stay committed and focus on a good shot.

Pitching

One of Susan's favorite pitch shots is the flop shot. She suggests playing this shot with a sand wedge. The arch of the swing is steeper than usual, creating a high, lofted shot and a soft landing with little roll. She feels that it is imperative to keep the arms and body moving together in the follow-through and says that the club will do the work if you keep moving and keep your grip pressure soft. The idea is to carry the ball close to the hole in the air and have little roll.

Susan says that the pitch shot, which should be used when hitting to an uphill green, is more like bump and run. As this will have a lower flight, she notes that there is more arm extension on the back and forward swing. She also states that it's always better to leave the ball a little short of the hole on an uphill pitch than to run it past and have a difficult putt coming back down the hill.

> The club will do the work if you keep moving and keep your grip pressure soft.

Bunker Shots

Around the green, Susan says, bunker shots can be fun. It's the only time in golf you shouldn't try to hit the ball. She says to keep your eyes focused on the sand about 1 inch behind the ball, which is where the club should enter the sand. The sand should splash out of the sand, as water would. Susan recommends opening the clubface for good lies and soft sand and closing the clubface for bad lies and hard or wet sand. As with the flop shots, she notes, your body and arms must keep moving forward.

The Mental Aspect

Susan's suggestion for the mental side of the game is first, to make an intelligent observation of the conditions and what shot will work best, and second, to draw from your experience and, of course, common sense. If you do this analysis properly and choose the correct club and type of shot to play, she says, your confidence will grow and you'll feel more mentally prepared.

Susan feels that pressure is self-induced, noting that no one really cares about your swing except you. Other golfers are too worried about their own swing and their own game.

8

Bill Whaley

Director of Golf, Tournament Players Club at River Highlands

Background for Learning

Bill has learned that any skill takes patience and effort, so he tries in his teaching to relate golf to other activities you have had success with. He notes that there is always that feeling of satisfaction when you improve your performance in a new activity, whether it's playing golf or painting a picture, so he suggests that you use memories of that feeling of improvement to help build confidence in your golf game. The gist of this approach is that you can carry that sense of accomplishment over to your golf game.

Bill also feels that it's very important to figure out the best learning situation for you individually. For example, you may prefer a class rather than a one-on-one experience, finding that you are able to relax, comprehend, and

Bill Whaley is the Director of Golf at the Tournament Players Club at River Highlands in Cromwell, Connecticut. Bill oversees all of the TPC golf courses in the Northeast. Bill's wife, Suzy Whaley, is one of the finest women club professional players in the country. She was the first woman to qualify for a PGA Tour event, the Greater Hartford Open, in fifty years.

The Tournament Players Club is the annual site for the Greater Hartford Open, one of the oldest events on the PGA schedule. The last four holes at the Tournament Players Club at River Highlands play around a lake, producing some of the most dramatic finishes on the PGA Tour.

perform better when you are in a more social situation. So he suggests that you take lessons in the environment that best suits your learning style.

According to Bill, many people don't understand that golf is a hard game. They see it on TV and it looks effortless, but then again, he notes, so does ballet. When learning to play, Bill says that your goal should be to establish good, solid fundamentals so that you know the most efficient way to play a given stroke.

> Your goal should be to establish good, solid fundamentals so that you know the most efficient way to play a given stroke.

Putting

One of the concepts Bill emphasizes when teaching golf is that you have to learn cause and effect to be able to improve. When putting, he recommends that you look at what happened and evaluate it. For example, why was the ball putted too far? Because the stroke was too big. The correction would be to measure the size of the stroke. If the size of the stroke is 10 inches back on the backstroke and 10 inches past the ball on the forward stroke, you should reduce the size of the swing somewhat. Maybe the size of the stroke becomes 8 inches on the backstroke and 8 inches on the forward stroke. Another example is why did the ball go to the left of the hole? Because the putter was aimed to the left. The correction in this case is to have a golfing partner stand behind the line of the putt and help you square the putter blade at the address position. Bill stresses that understanding the cause and effect of your shots puts you in charge of the results.

Bill then leaves it to the individual player to take ownership of results. Did you miss that 3-foot putt because of technique or because of nerves? If you missed the putt because your technique was not good, then you should ask your teacher for instruction on technique. If nerves was the cause, you should ask for strategies for calming down before you putt, such as deep breathing exercises and a good preshot routine.

According to Bill, putting is a simple endeavor and does not need a lot of information, but it does require some clear communication with your instructor in the learning process. Bill feels that you should give putting a good try and then, with some solid adjustments from your teacher, you will start to develop the correct technique. Bill tailors his instruction around the feedback that students give him, rather than some hard-and-fast set of rules. This feedback makes you a partner in the learning process, with you and your teacher working together. Bill feels that a good teacher-student relationship is like a doctor-patient relationship, that a certain trust and commitment is developed. This gives you the confidence to ask better questions, which helps both you and your teacher achieve the goal of game improvement.

As for the anxiety that sometimes accompanies putting, Bill notes that everyone experiences some nervousness when putting, even the PGA Tour stars. Bill reminds you that a good way to stay calm is to reflect on calmer times, times when you are extremely relaxed, such as reading a good book in bed or relaxing in front of a warm fireplace. Reflecting on those times will lower your heart rate and blood pressure a notch and give you a good chance to perform at your best.

Chipping

Bill teaches what he calls the "one-lever system" for chipping, in which you basically putt the ball with a middle iron. Bill suggests that you experiment with different clubs (normally a 6 or a 7 iron)

The "one-lever system" around the greens is a very reliable method to play chip and short pitch shots. Use your putting grip, which will reduce any wrist hinge, then swing the club with your arms and shoulders, similar to a putting stroke.

to find the one that feels best to you. Use a long putting-type stroke with no wrist hinge and a simple shoulder and arm swing, as seen in the sequence above.

Bills finds that the advantage of this system is that the ball is almost always on target and the line is automatic. Because the one-lever stroke is so simple and there are no moving parts, solid contact is assured. It is a guarantee that you will hit the ball on the green and on line.

> Because the one-lever stroke is so simple and there are no moving parts, solid contact is assured.

Pitching

Bill finds that one of the most common mistakes that the recreational golfer faces when making pitch shots, whether 20 yards or 60 yards, is using too much swing, resulting in the ball flying across the green. He notes that the pitching wedge, the club designed for this shot, creates a shot where the ball goes about two thirds of the way to the hole in the air and rolls the last third. It's a simple concept, but one many golfers complicate by trying to fly the ball too far to the hole.

Bill says that you should keep it simple and just allow for the normal flight and roll of the ball to the flagstick. To do this, he suggests that you pick a reasonable landing spot. Picture the ball in the air and then take a good guess as to how much it will roll. Make a mental note of where you want to land the ball and take a practice swing that will produce enough force to land the ball there. Bill notes that if the ball lands on that spot and ends up near the hole, that is a job well done. If it finishes short or long of the hole, it is a learning experience, and next time you'll adjust the landing spot.

> Bill says that you should keep it simple and just allow for the normal flight and roll of the ball to the flagstick.

Bunker Shots

When teaching bunker shots, Bill sells the idea that "this isn't as hard as I thought." That point alone will bring down some of your blood pressure and anxiety. He feels that the best way to understand the concept of the bunker shot is to draw lines in the practice bunker so that you can see the subtle changes in technique that you have to have to be successful. Bill will first draw a line in the sand to show the line toward the target. Second, Bill will draw a line to demonstrate opening the stance, a line across the toes that should point to the left of the target (for right-handed players). Bill will draw the third line to show where the ball is positioned relative to the stance. For a good lie, that position will be forward. If the ball is in a hole or is depressed, that position will be more toward the back foot.

To improve your bunker shot, Bill offers these adjustments to your technique:

1. Open your stance slightly (a line across the toes aims slightly to the left of the target for right-handed players).
2. The clubhead should enter the sand about 2 inches behind the ball.
3. The clubhead doesn't hit the ball itself but throws a divot of sand and the ball onto the green.

One suggestion Bill has for the mental side of the bunker shot is to relax and just try to get the ball on the green. Bill notes that we see great players on the PGA Tour hitting bunker shots at the flagstick as though they were throwing darts at a dartboard, but that's just unrealistic for most average golfers. If you are a recreational player, however, you are way ahead of the game if you can get the ball on the green, so Bill advises that you relax, take a deep breath, take a good swing, and knock that divot of sand and the ball somewhere on the green.

> Relax, take a deep breath, take a good swing, and knock that divot of sand and the ball somewhere on the green.

The Mental Aspect

Bill has some great ideas about enjoying the game and improving your mind-set. His first suggestion is to be your own "best friend" when you play. So often we miss a short putt, leave the ball in the bunker, or just badly misplay a shot we know we can play. It's so easy to get down on ourselves with negative self-talk and negative thoughts. If a real-life best friend were present, he says, they would tell us that we should forget what happened, that everyone hits a poor shot from time to time, and that we should move on and stay positive. Being your own best friend makes sense and will keep you positive for the rest of the round.

Bill's second suggestion is to schedule more lessons either on the course or in practice areas that are similar to the course. He finds that it is much easier to absorb new information when you're on the course itself—after all, the course is where you play. It's more the "real world" of golf. Being on the course with your teacher affords you the opportunity to face your fears with the person who can really help. For instance, there may be a situation on the course that always causes you difficulty, maybe it's a carry over water or a severe downhill lie. The best way to improve your score and, as Bill says, "get that monkey off your back," is to address those problems straight on with your teacher. This also underscores his point that you and your teacher should be frank and friendly—the "we're in this together" approach will achieve the best results.

Bill's third suggestion is to "stay in the game." Train yourself to stay positive. You know that you'll have your share of good shots and bad shots, good bounces and bad bounces. The game is a process that develops over nine or eighteen holes, he says, so you have to be patient and know that even when the game is not going well, there is a pretty good chance that the day will improve. Stay in the game so good things—better scores and shots—will come your way.

To achieve this, Bill suggests that you give equal weight and effort to each shot. A 10-foot putt for birdie is just as important as a 10-foot putt for a bogey—it is just a 10-foot putt. Whether for birdie or bogey, the shot affects our score the same amount, and assigning different values will create unnecessary stress. This will not help you relax and stay on an even keel.

> A 10-foot putt for birdie is just as important as a 10-foot putt for a bogey—it is just a 10-foot putt.

A fourth suggestion that Bill offers is to encourage you to have a slightly different mind-set when you practice. Think of the practice sessions more as a rehearsal than a practice. Have good goals and hold yourself accountable. For example, Bill suggests that when you practice chipping, use ten balls with the goal of having four out of ten within 3 feet of the hole. Of course, he notes, the goals will vary with your ability levels. For example, a new player's goal may be two out of ten within 3 feet of the hole, but for a low-handicap player, it may be eight out of ten within 3 feet of the hole. But, he emphasizes, you should have that type of challenge, noting that practicing with goals will help you focus more, just as you should on the course. If you hold yourself accountable, he says, it will give you a better idea of your real proficiency and a way to identify areas that need the most improvement. And, he notes, taking that information to your teacher will certainly make the next lesson more productive.

Bill's final and fun suggestion is to change the dynamics of the game somewhat, to stay creative and see your course in a different light. If you've played the white tees for a long time, try one round from the red tees and one round from the blue tees. Try playing from the 150-yard marker in to the hole to mix it up a little. Simple changes like this will give you better insight into your game's strengths and weaknesses, and it's fun!

9

Joe Rehor

Director of Golf, Bethpage Golf Course

Putting

When teaching putting, Joe likes to start with a fundamental lesson on alignment. Joe points out that all golf balls have lettering that states the brand name and that this lettering forms a line on the ball. After you mark the ball, replace the ball on the green so that the lettering is aimed directly down the line of the putt toward the hole. Joe states that using the lettering on the ball guarantees good alignment. He says that this is a good habit to get into when you play and one that Tiger Woods uses.

Joe's next step in teaching putting is to achieve the correct address position. He feels that many players stand too far from the ball, making it difficult to "see" the line and to keep the putter blade square to the hole. He recom-

Joe Rehor is the Director of Golf at the Bethpage Golf Course in Farmingdale, New York. Joe was captain of the St. John's golf team in his amateur days. He has received the Metropolitan PGA Merchandiser of the Year Award. Joe has also been a leader in junior golf, both in teaching and organizing tournaments. Joe can always be found on the lesson tee at Bethpage and is one of the best teachers on Long Island.

There are five great golf courses at Bethpage: the Yellow, the Blue, the Red, the Green, and the Black. The Black Course was the venue for the 2002 U.S. Open won by Tiger Woods and will host the U.S. Open again in 2009.

mends standing close enough at address to have your eyes directly over the ball. Joe finds that the advantages of this approach are threefold:

1. You can easily see the line of the putt as you move your head from side to side.
2. It makes it easy to swing the putter straight back and straight through.
3. You will achieve the exact same address position each time, which is the first step to being consistent.

Joe thinks that in the correct address position, if you were to draw an imaginary line from the hands down to the ball, the ball would be underneath the front hand (the left hand if you are right-handed, the right hand if you are left-handed). Basically, this puts your hands slightly ahead of the clubhead, which helps keep the hands working as one unit. He also notes that your grip pressure on the handle of the putter should be soft.

Joe feels that the putting stroke should be a combination of arms and shoulders swinging the putter, with no or very little hand action. Joe's most important tip on the stroke is that you shouldn't decelerate the swing with the putter. Decelerating the putter will create an open or closed face, and the putt will most likely not reach the hole.

Joe's advice for those who have recently had the putting woes is to try a belly putter. The belly putter will give you the "feel" back without being as extreme as the long putter. After using the belly putter a little while, he says, you may want to go back to the standard-length putter but that "sometimes a change of scenery will do you good."

> After you mark the ball, replace the ball on the green so that the lettering is aimed directly down the line of the putt toward the hole.

Chipping

When teaching chipping, Joe first recommends that you develop an awareness of how far the ball flies in the air and how much it rolls on the green in the chip shot. Figuring out how much airtime and how much roll the ball makes takes some experience, so you will need to practice. He also suggests that you visualize what spot on the green the ball should land on and then visualize it rolling toward the hole.

For stance, Joe recommends that you stand as close to the ball as you would if you were putting. The club you chip with will not be able to sit flat on the ground but will sit somewhat on the toe of the club. He suggests playing the chip with a 9 iron or a pitching wedge. He recommends these more lofted clubs, he says, because most players hit the ball too hard when they are close to the green, often sailing the ball over the green, but the loft of the pitching wedge or 9 iron will limit the amount of roll. He also provides a simple technique for making the stroke: "brush" the grass during the practice swing. He says that this brushing action is the best possible chipping stroke because the clubhead stays low to the ground, making solid contact almost a given.

Pitching

For pitch shots, Joe recommends that you use the pitching wedge in most cases, and the gap wedge and sand wedge if needed. He hardly ever recommends the 60-degree wedge, saying that the 60-degree wedge is only for the professional player. He feels it just has too much "downside" in that a poor shot will be a disaster.

Joe uses an interesting technique in teaching this shot—listening. He suggests that you listen to the swish that the correct swing will make. When the club is swung properly, it will just graze the top of the grass, making the swishing sound. If the club is swung incorrectly, the clubhead will dig into the ground, creating a rather dull thud. It's a fun way to improve!

In the pitch shot, you swing the club from about waist high in back to waist high in front. On the follow-through, Joe thinks that the face of the club should point to the sky, which is different from the regular swing, when the toe of the club points to the sky. This type of finish produces a swing where the clubhead is not "released." While Joe realizes that this concept may seem a little technical and geared toward advanced players, simply put, the clubface stays open longer than on the standard swing.

Bunker Shots

Once again, Joe likes to rely on his listening technique when teaching the bunker shot. During practice, swing the club in the bunker so that the clubhead sends a divot of sand out of the bunker and on to the green. The clubhead sliding through the sand will make a splashing sound. He feels that practicing this listening technique is a great way to learn the correct feel and correct amount of sand to be displaced for this shot.

Joe teaches that to properly play the greenside bunker shot, you must learn how to use the bounce of the wedge. The bounce, or flange, is the extra metal on the bottom of the clubface of the sand wedge that helps the club slide through and not dig into the sand.

Joe has a great story to describe how to best use the bounce of a sand wedge. A Scottish golf pro told him, "You'll never learn

He suggests that you listen to the swish that the correct swing will make. When the club is swung properly, it will just graze the top of the grass, making the swishing sound.

SHORT GAME SECRETS OF THE PROS

Joe Rehor teaches a pitch shot with the face of the club pointing toward the sky on the follow-through. This method produces a high, soft shot.

The "bounce" of the wedge allows the clubhead to slide through the sand. This sliding effect will help throw a divot of sand and the ball onto the green.

how to hit a bunker shot until you can do this: Bury a dollar bill about an inch deep in the sand, just about where the divot of sand would be on your bunker shot. Set the ball in the sand about in the area the dollar bill would be (if you could see the bill). Swing the clubhead, skimming the sand so that the ball and the sand come out of the bunker and the bill stays in the bunker." It's a neat trick. It may cost you a few dollars, but it's worth it!

10

Gil McNally

Director of Golf, Garden City Golf Club

Gil McNally is the Director of Golf at Garden City Golf Club in Garden City, New York. Gil was awarded the Metropolitan PGA Teacher of the Year Award in 1991.

The Garden City Golf Club has been on every Top 100 course list every year. It is a beautiful links-style layout with a rich history.

Putting

When teaching putting, Gil emphasizes that putting is not rocket science, it's just rolling a ball toward a hole. Thus, it should be kept as simple as possible. Gil teaches that success is a product of good visualization and good hand-eye coordination. He believes that we all possess the ability to putt the ball reasonably well.

Gil emphasizes that the speed at which we putt the ball dictates the line. If the putt is going fast, it will break less than one that has not been hit so hard. Thus, control over the ball's speed is essential to good putting. And control over the speed is a product of "feel," which you can only achieve with practice. You need to develop a sense of how much power each size putting stroke will create.

> For the short ones, keep your head still and the blade square.

If there is a secret to making those elusive short putts, Gil thinks that it is to start with the putter blade square to the hole and to keep it square during the stroke. For the short ones, keep your head still and the blade square.

Chipping

For chipping, Gil likes to teach what is called the Paul Runyan Method. This method, developed by one of the true masters of the short game, recommends that the chip-shot stroke is played almost identical to the putting stroke. With this method, Gil says to:

1. Stand as close to the ball at address as you do when putting.
2. Set the chipping iron on the ground so that it sits on the toe.
3. Use a putting stroke with a mid iron (a 4, 5, 6, or 7), not a putter.
4. Change the height of the shot by alternating the lofts of the clubs you use.

Pitching

Gil describes Garden City Golf Club as having U.S. Open–like conditions almost all of the time. The greens there are firm and fast and are surrounded by long grass, which is very difficult to play from. For that reason, Gil teaches a fairly big, flowing swing on pitch shots around the green, which produces a soft shot. This style suits this type of course well. He notes that you will also see this style of play when you look at the LPGA and PGA tour professionals. Probably the best proponent of this style is Phil Mickelson. He can appear to take a full, slow swing on a 30-yard shot and have the ball land ever so gently on the green. To develop this shot, Gil says, "you must feel with your hands," noting that it is impossible and unrealistic to rely on mechanical moves or positions to dictate or control distance. You have to rely on good visualization and then trust that you will make the correct size swing to match the distance.

At the address position, Gil teaches that you should pull the left foot back, which opens the stance and preclears the shoulders. Your arms and shoulders swing together away from

Gil McNally teaches the simple "pitch as you putt" system. Gil chooses a mid iron (4 to 7 iron, depending on the desired trajectory), and addresses the ball exactly as he would with a putter.

The stroke for the pitch shot is the same as a long putting stroke. Your wrists do not hinge, and the club is swung by your arms and shoulders. Notice that Gil's head stays steady throughout the stroke.

and toward the target. He says that the feeling should be that of your arms following your shoulders.

Gil's other tips for pitch shots are twofold. First, your grip pressure should be light, about a three on a scale of one to ten. And second, to adjust the height of the shot, adjust the ball position. Thus, for low shots, the ball should be back in the stance; for medium-height shots, the ball is in the middle of the stance; and for high shots, the ball is forward in the stance.

Gil discusses the importance of properly identifying how the ball sits in the grass to correctly play a pitch shot. To execute a high shot around the green, he says, the first step is to evaluate the lie. To hit the ball high, it must be sitting "up" in the grass to some degree, to give it a little air underneath (somewhat like having a small tee under the ball). The second step is to use a lofted wedge, a sand wedge, a 60-degree wedge, or a lob wedge. The best club to use for most of these strokes is the sand wedge, he says. If the shot calls for an extremely high shot, you would then choose the 60-degree or lob wedge. The third step is to play the ball forward in the stance. And the fourth step is to keep the clubface square to the target during the stroke.

> The ball should be forward in the stance, and the stance should be a little wider than normal to promote stability.

Bunker Shots

Gil feels that the bunker shot should be played from an open stance, meaning that the line across the toes points to the left of the target for right-handed players. The ball should be forward in the stance, and the stance should be a little wider than normal to promote stability. As in all golf swings, he says, the body must keep moving, for this is a shot that requires a good swing. The clubface should remain open through the hitting area. Gil notes that you will feel the club glide through the sand because of the extra metal on the sole of the club, which prevents it from digging into the sand.

Lastly, Gil emphasizes that a full follow-through is the key to throwing a divot of sand and the ball on to the green.

11

Keith Maxwell

Head Professional, Sunningdale Golf Club

Putting

When coaching putting, Keith says that a key to success in putting the ball at a course like Sunningdale is to keep the putter blade low throughout the stroke. This will help the ball hug the ground on the way to the hole. He notes that if the ball bounces at all on greens that are windy, it will most certainly be thrown off line. This technique is the best way to putt on any course in any part of the world. As Sunningdale is a typical links and seaside course, this method of having the ball roll purely and not bounce is exaggerated.

Keith Maxwell is the head professional at Sunningdale Golf Club in Surrey County, England, just miles southwest of London. Keith, a Scotsman, is only the seventh professional in the club's history.

Sunningdale is one of the finest courses in Europe. It was designed by the legendary British player Willie Park Jr. in 1901. It has a great history and hosted the Walker Cup in 1987, the European Open in 1987, and the Ladies British Open in 1987, 2001, and 2004.

Chipping

Keith says that the lies at a course like Sunningdale are very tight (defined as the ball being on ground that has so little grass that it is like playing the ball off bare ground), particularly during the summer and autumn. This is a condition we all experience at our own courses when the ball settles in an area that has received a lot of traffic either by foot or by golf carts. Thus, he thinks that a low, running chip shot is by far the most effective shot for getting the ball close to the hole in such a situation. He notes that the shot that will catch your eye in this circumstance is the lob shot, but that is very difficult to do. And even when you do manage to time the ball perfectly and get a good strike with the turf, the ball will spin uncontrollably. This leaves you a long chip shot from the hole. Rather than playing the high shot, Keith feels that a much better approach is a chip shot. To play this, you need to hit down on the ball and pinch it against the turf.

Keith states that although the club you use to chip around the green should vary depending upon the amount of roll you require, you should stick with about a 7, an 8, or a 9 iron. The club Keith recommends most is the 7 iron because it is reliable and because once you get used to it you'll be able to control the distance. Keith prefers that the style of the swing be much like a putting stroke, with firm wrists and no hand action.

> The club Keith recommends most is the 7 iron because it is reliable and because once you get used to it you'll be able to control the distance.

Bunker Shots

Keith tells his students that all courses have bunkers that have different texture sand. On some courses, the sand is light and fluffy, while at others, the sand is heavy. Keith says that when you are dealing with a bunker where the sand is firm to heavy, the shot requires a bold and confident swing. He notes that it is important to understand how to play the stroke and then confidently make a good swing. A tentative shot will leave you in the bunker. He also reiterates the importance of a good follow-through in the bunker.

Shots from the Rough

If your ball is caught in the rough, Keith notes that difficult grass or heather has a nasty way of grabbing your clubface at impact and turning the face shut. To counter this, he thinks that you need a lot of speed and a stronger grip than normal to even get the ball airborne from the rough. Keith's tip for the shot from the deep and nasty rough is to address the ball with the clubface slightly open, not much, just a degree or two. Slightly opening the face at address will somewhat counter the effect that the rough has of shutting the clubface. And while Keith never recommends gripping the club too tightly, he does feel for this stroke that you should slightly increase your grip pressure to minimize the twisting effect of the long grass or heather.

He recommends asking the course's professional if the greens tend to break a certain way, noting that that question alone can save you many strokes along the way.

Reading the Course

Keith says that as a rule, the Old Course greens and most greens on links courses have subtle undulations and are mostly overread. You get what you see with them. There is no underlying pull for the breaks, such as water or a valley. He realizes, however, that this underlying pull may exist at a course you often play, particularly if the course is in the mountains. Thus, he recommends asking the course's professional if the greens tend to break a certain way, noting that that question alone can save you many strokes along the way. And if you play at Sunningdale or any links course, he says, "don't read too much into the break, go with your first impression, and you'll have a good day on the greens."

12

John Schob

Head Professional, Huntington Crescent Club

The Short Game

While playing college golf for Rutgers, John felt that what he lacked in length could be more than made up for by a solid short game. As a teacher, he now specializes in the short game, feeling that it is the aspect of the game that gives him the chance to help his students the most. His technique is particularly well suited to the championship-like conditions at his course.

Putting

According to John, confidence is the most important trait that you need to putt well. Thus, if you are a new player, he likes to begin

John Schob is the head professional at the Huntington Crescent Club on the north shore of Long Island, New York. John was president of the Metropolitan PGA from 1990 to 1993 and has been selected for several awards, the most prestigious of which is Professional of the Year for the Metropolitan PGA in 1993. He has been the professional at the Crescent Club since 1976.

The Huntington Crescent Club was the site of the Rheingold Invitational in the 1950s, which drew all of the great players of that era, such as Sam Snead, Tommy Bolt, Ken Venturi, and many others.

lessons with a 1-foot putt to start out on that confident note. After you make some of the very short ones, he has you move back to develop a little longer stroke and a feel for distance. John feels that it's also a good idea for newer players to play some minor competitions to keep interest and get a feel for the game itself. For more experienced golfers, he suggests that the road to regained confidence may be different, particularly if you feel like you have lost your touch. John says that a good step to regain confidence is to try using the long putter. The long putter is a totally different approach and often will help hide those negative thoughts that have crept in over time.

John feels that it is very important to choose the correct length putter. If you are using a long putter, he recommends that the handle of the putter should rest against the middle of your chest.

The long putter has saved more than one golf career. John Schob demonstrates the correct address position with the long putter. The handle of the putter should comfortably rest on your chest and your forward elbow should be aimed at the hole.

After using the long putter for a while, you may be able to go back to the standard putter and find that it feels great. John says that he doesn't know why this is so, but that's golf. Another great trick he mentions, particularly if you are a good player who has lost your feel, is to close your eyes when you putt. He acknowledges that it's a little off the beaten track but says that it has worked for many good players, some of whom will admit to it and many others who will not.

If the long putter is not working, John recommends that you engage in a good amount of trial and error to come up with a feel that is different and better. One variation he suggests is the claw grip. In the claw, he says, you keep the top hand the same as you would for your regular putting grip, but you change the position of the bottom hand, gripping the putter handle in the space between your thumb and

With the long putter, your bottom hand swings the putter while your top hand keeps the handle of the club anchored against the chest. There is a minimum of moving parts, making the long putter a good option when the regular-length putter is not working well.

forefinger and laying the fingers on the top of the shaft. The effect of this grip is that the bottom hand is less active during the stroke, which promotes a smoother swing.

Another variation John suggests is to use the cross-handed grip. To achieve the cross-handed grip, simply reverse your hands on the grip. This produces a very different feel. John notes that the advantage to this grip is that it prevents any wrist action, which is the cause of so many missed putts along the way. When using this stroke, he says that you actually pull the club down the line toward the hole with the bottom hand. It's a simple, one-piece action. John says that Gary Player and Arnold Palmer were asked, at different times, if they had one thing to change about their games what

Confidence is the most important trait that you need to putt well.

it would be. They both said that they would putt cross-handed. Now that's a pretty good endorsement.

John's first checkpoint when teaching putting is to make sure that your putter blade is square to the hole, meaning that the clubface is at a 90-degree angle to the hole. If the putter is not aimed properly at the hole, he says, there is very little chance that the ball will be on line. A good teaching tool John employs to ensure a square clubface is the laser training putter—a laser pointer is attached to the putter blade and sends a laser beam showing exactly where the putter is aimed. His next checkpoint is making sure that you swing the putter on the correct path—straight back and straight through.

John's approach is thus to keep it as simple as possible: proper alignment, followed by proper path.

> John's approach is thus to keep it as simple as possible: proper alignment, followed by proper path.

Chipping

John learned his teaching technique for chipping and pitching from the legendary Paul Runyon. Runyon was a true master of the short game and a "giant killer" during his time on the PGA Tour. In the 1938 PGA Championship at Shawnee on the Delaware, for example, Sam Snead consistently out drove Runyon by over 50 yards every hole, only to lose that championship to Runyon's mastery of the short game. John explains that Runyon's style minimizes hand action and relies on the arms and shoulders to swing the club.

John feels that most players have overactive hands and release (or throw) the clubhead too early, causing missed hits and generally poor contact. In the correct action, he says, you make a slight alteration in the grip so that both palms are pointing skyward.

This locks your hands into a neutral position and makes any wrist action or hinging almost impossible. From this address position, you swing the arms and shoulders with no wrist hinge. He notes that it's the same feeling as "rocking a baby." The clubface stays square to the target throughout the swing and never changes, very similar to the arm- and shoulder-type putting stroke.

Pitching

John carries this same Runyon method over to the longer 20- to 60-yard pitch shots. Once again, he says, when gripping your club, your palms face the sky and there is little or no wrist action. This style relies on the bigger muscles of the arms and shoulders, not on the smaller muscles of the hands. To hit the ball a little farther, John suggests increasing the size of the swing.

Given a fairly clean lie, he says, where the ball is sitting some-what "up" in the grass (not nestled down), this method will pro-duce a lofted pitch shot that will land ever so softly on the green. You can quickly develop a feel for how far the ball will carry and roll because the ball has little or no spin. If the ball is not lying cleanly in the grass but is nestled down to some degree, John sug-gests that you change your stance so that the ball position is back center. This change of stance will create a steeper angle on the downswing and allow you to hit down on the ball. He notes that the downward pressure of the clubhead and the loft of the club will pop the ball out of that nestled down lie and up onto the green.

When practicing pitch shots, John suggests using at least three different clubs, such as a lob wedge, a pitching wedge, and a 7 iron, around the green to give yourself a good variety of shots to play. While he says that you should determine which three clubs to use, they should give you a good variety of loft and options. For a course with fairly small greens in championship condition, such as the Huntington Crescent Club, John suggests learning to use the lob wedge. He admits that this club requires some homework, but says that it really will pay off on a course of this style.

Bunker Shots

For a course like the Huntington Crescent Club, which has small, deep bunkers and rather small greens, John recommends playing sand shots with a lob wedge. It has more loft and helps get the ball up quickly. With the lob wedge, he notes, you don't have to open the stance as you do with the normal sand wedge shot; the lob wedge has plenty of loft built in, so you don't need to open the stance for additional height.

To play the bunker shot properly, John teaches that you have to feel the bounce of the wedge. The bounce, or flange on the bottom of the clubface, helps the clubhead slide through the sand. If you make a swing with the club in the sand and let the bounce work properly, he says, you'll hear a "swish." John teaches that that certain sound and the feel of the club sliding through and not digging into the sand are key to learning the use of the bounce and the first step in becoming a good wedge player.

On a more technical note, when teaching bunker shots, John teaches that the lower part of the body should remain quiet. John wants you to set your feet and to then make the swing, mostly with your arms and shoulders, without a lot of weight transfer or leg action to complicate the shot. He teaches that you should focus on moving the sand, because it is the divot of sand and the cushion of sand behind the ball that throw the ball out of the bunker and onto the green, and says that you should not be concerned with the ball. He realizes that it's easy to be overly conscious of the ball rather than of moving the divot of sand from the bunker to the green and suggests that you imagine the ball to be just another particle of sand that is coming out of the bunker along with the rest of the sand divot.

John passes along one final tip for bunker shots. If you are faced with a sand shot that requires a lot of loft, a change that he suggests is to "weaken" your top hand grip so that the "V" on that hand points more toward your nose than it does to your back shoulder. This change in grip ensures that the clubface will remain open throughout the shot and thus that you'll have maximum loft on that particular shot.

13

Jay Horton

Head Professional, Philadelphia Country Club

Putting

Jay credits much of his teaching about putting to Todd Sones, who has a great reputation for teaching PGA and LPGA professionals the art of putting. The most important ingredient in his technique is to properly fit the student to the correct length putter. He says that the most efficient way to build a repeating putting stroke is to be able to extend your arms at address, and you can't extend your arms if the putter is too long. Jay asked a leading club manufacturer why most putters seem too long for his students and the answer was "that the putters fit better in the bag at that length." Not a good answer. The net result, Jay feels, is that most golfers putt with a putter that is too long.

Jay Horton is the head professional at the Philadelphia Country Club. Jay has also been the head professional at the Rockaway Hunting Club in Lawrence, New York, and at the Detroit Golf Club in Detroit, Michigan. Jay also was a very successful player on the European Senior Tour.

Philadelphia Country Club has been the site of many USGA events. It was the course at which Sam Snead lost his best chance to win the 1939 U.S. Open by making a triple bogey on the last hole, which was then a relatively easy par 5. The eventual winner was Byron Nelson, who beat Denny Shute and Craig Wood in a playoff.

> He says that the most efficient way to build a repeating putting stroke is to be able to extend your arms at address, and you can't extend your arms if the putter is too long.

To putt correctly, according to Jay, you should be comfortable, in good posture, with your eyes over the ball and your arms extended. To achieve this position, Jay feels that the average length of a putter should be about 32 or 33 inches rather than the current 34 or 35 inches. This may seem like a small point, he says, but to create a true pendulum stroke, the arms should be extended at the address position and that's impossible if the putter is not the correct (and short) length. Jay says that the setup is everything—if you are in the correct starting position, it's easy to make a good putting stroke. If your starting position is not correct, you wind up compensating throughout the putting stroke.

Chipping and Pitching

For both the chip shot and the pitch shot, Jay believes that your hands should be ahead of the clubhead at impact. He points out that this is true in all shots and that perfect form during the swing or stroke is not the requirement, but rather that the position at impact on all shots is what really matters. To illustrate this, Jay uses Bruce Lietzke and Jim Furyk as examples. Both have unorthodox styles all the way through their games, from the driver to the chip shot, but they have been extremely successful and durable through their careers because their impact positions have been correct. Jay's point is that all great players look the same at impact, with their hands ahead of the ball. To emphasize this point, Jay suggests teeing up the ball on a chip or pitch shot and trying to hit the tee rather than the ball. This exercise forces you to hit slightly downward on the ball. This is exactly the effect Jay is trying to create. This slightly downward action is what ensures solid contact and allows the loft of the club to lift the ball, whether it be a chip shot or a full iron from the fairway.

Jay thinks that many players try to lift the chip and pitch shots—it's human nature to try to help the ball into the air. If the clubhead is lifted at the bottom of the swing, it will strike the middle or equator of the ball and it will go scurrying across the green. The bottom of the club must hit the bottom of the ball to achieve any loft.

The technique Jay suggests to overcome this tendency is to address the ball with a "Y" position at address. In this position, your hands are slightly ahead of the ball and an imaginary line drawn across your shoulders and arms would create the letter "Y." He then says to move the entire "Y" when hitting the chip shot, with no wrist break. As you move off the green and the length of the shot goes from the chip to the pitch shot, you need to increase the size of the swing, but Jay cautions that there should be little or no wrist hinge until the clubhead reaches waist high on the swing. Before that, he suggests, somewhat jokingly, that you duct-tape your wrist so that there is no wrist break. When the swing reaches waist high, there should be a hint of some wrist hinge or break. Naturally, he says, there has to be some good timing and feel to go along with all this technical movement.

> Jay suggests teeing up the ball on a chip or pitch shot and trying to hit the tee rather than the ball. This exercise forces you to hit slightly downward on the ball.

Jay emphasizes that in the chip and pitch shots, the ball should be struck on the downswing. The slight downward path of the club and the loft of the club are what get the ball airborne. Your hands should always be slightly ahead of the clubhead at impact to ensure solid contact. He also says that the head of the club should swing straight back and straight through. The clubhead should swing on the line of flight, never inside that line.

For club selection around the greens, Jay suggests three clubs—the 8 iron, the pitching wedge, and the sand wedge. Situations change daily, but his basic formulas are these: the 8 iron will make the ball fly one third of the way in the air and roll the other two thirds; the pitching wedge will carry the ball halfway in the air and will roll it the other half; and the sand wedge will carry the ball three quarters of the distance in the air and roll it the last quarter. Jay is not a big fan of the lob wedge for most recreational golfers, simply because you have to generate too much clubhead speed to hit the ball hard enough to reach the hole. He says that swinging hard from a short distance makes control difficult. Short shots are finesse shots and you should not feel that there is any problem reaching the hole. He also notes that swinging hard will result in the dreaded "thin" shot, when you strike the ball at the equator and it sails over the green. Instead, Jay suggests using the pitching wedge in most cases and the sand wedge if you need a high, soft shot.

Bunker Shots

Jay says that all golfers know that one of the most difficult shots in the game is the long bunker shot. To execute this shot correctly, Jay says that you want to have the clubhead enter the sand 1½ to 2 inches behind the ball, but you have to swing hard to reach the hole. The sand acts as a cushion, and it takes a lot of clubhead speed to hit the ball 60 or 70 feet.

Jay's tip to increase your chance of success on longer bunker shots is to address the ball as you normally would in the bunker, then move your feet back about

> Jay's tip to increase your chance of success on longer bunker shots is to address the ball as you normally would in the bunker, then move your feet back about an inch so you are standing a little farther from the ball than you normally would.

an inch so you are standing a little farther from the ball than you normally would. He says that this slight adjustment will keep the clubhead shallow as it enters the sand, making it a lot easier to move the divot of sand and the ball onto the green. A more shallow swing will also prevent the clubhead from digging too deeply

The long greenside bunker shot (around 75 feet) requires a full swing. A good thought is to swing about the same as you would with a full pitching wedge from the fairway.

into the sand. He notes that if the clubhead digs, you will not be able to generate enough speed to move the divot of sand and the ball a long way.

The Mental Aspect

Jay feels that the most important quality you can have to be a good player is a positive mental attitude. He notes that it is easy to get down on yourself, particularly when you miss a very short putt or hit a shot that is so bad that you can't believe you hit it. We all do miss shots like that—even the best players in the world will, every now and then, hit one so badly that they are in shock. On these occasions, Jay suggests that you be your own "best friend." What would your best friend say if he or she were with you? Jays says that your best friend would say something positive—how a good next shot can make up for the last poor one, how you're really a fine player, and all of the other things that good friends say to one another. So he recommends that when you get into the self-talk mode, be good to yourself and good things will happen.

> The best road to developing a champion mind-set and becoming the best you can be is to win early in whatever competition you are playing in.

Jay also has some good thoughts about building a champion. He feels that the best road to developing a champion mind-set and becoming the best you can be is to win early in whatever competition you are playing in. He notes that the winning attitude and mind-set is something that cannot be taught but must be experienced. The proof of this idea, he says, is personified in the career of Tom Kite, arguably the best all-around player in a period that stretched from the early 1980s to the mid-1990s. His only problem was that for a player of his talents, he simply did not win enough. He was the second-best young player at his course in Austin, and he was also the second-best young player in the country. The number one player at his club (and in the country) was a young man named Ben Crenshaw. Ben not only won the club championship but also the NCAA three times. Tom was always in the hunt, just that shot or two behind Ben in almost every event. Tom eventually did learn to win, with the highlight of his career being winning the U.S. Open at Pebble Beach, but Jay feels that he had to overcome his early career mind-set to achieve this.

Jay feels that once you get used to winning, it becomes easier the next time you play. Thus, a good step toward developing a champion mind-set is to play in events that you can win. This goes somewhat counter to the idea of "stepping up in class" to play against stiffer competition, but Jay feels that there is no substitute for that successful feeling of simply winning.

14

Jimmie Brothers

Director of Golf, Plantation Golf Resort

Putting

When he teaches putting, Jimmie has four keys. The first key is good alignment. According to Jimmie, the face of the putter must be square to the intended line of the putt. If the clubface does not start out squarely at the line, then you have to make an adjustment during the stroke, which, he notes, is impossible on a repeating basis. Second, he states that your eyes should be directly over the ball. Doing this ensures that you will be looking up and down the line. Third, when making the swing, Jimmie advises that you use minimal wrist action. Using the arms and shoulders rather than the wrist will produce a smoother, more repeatable putting stroke. And finally, Jimmie says to stay down throughout the stroke. In other words, the putter head should stay low to

Jimmie Brothers is Director of Golf at the Plantation Inn and Golf Resort in Crystal River, Florida. Jimmie started playing golf at the age of four and was a child star, winning the Florida Junior title at age fifteen. As a professional, Jimmie has received the coveted Teacher of the Year award from the South Florida Section of the PGA.

In the late 1950s and 1960s, many professionals practiced at Plantation Golf Resort before the Masters, which was held in mid-April. The pros would finish their West Coast swing in February and then head to Crystal River in early April. The weather was better in Crystal River, Florida, than it was in Augusta, Georgia—and the fishing was great!

the ground throughout the stroke—it is important to stay with the stroke until the ball is on its way.

Once you are comfortable with these keys, Jimmie says that the next step is to learn to control the distance. While there is really no substitute for experience in gauging how hard to hit a given putt, he suggests that you get a feel for how much of a stroke will produce a certain amount of roll on the ball. The length of the backstroke will determine how much power is created in the stroke. The longer the putting stroke, the farther the ball will roll.

One of Jimmie's tips about being a good short putter is really about alignment. After all, no player is really going to have trouble with how hard to hit the putt on a very short one. Jimmie stresses that you have to trust where you are aiming. One of the best ways to ensure proper alignment on the short ones is to aim the lettering on the ball to the hole, something you've probably seen Tiger Woods do. Once you have the letters lined up, Jimmie says, just go ahead and roll the ball down the line. If you missed a short putt, it's probably because you either didn't trust the line or you looked up too early to see where the ball ended up. As Jimmie says, it's about trust and good alignment.

Jimmie feels that bad putting, also known as the "yips," comes from too much hand action. He says that you should always try to quiet the little muscles of your hands and use the big muscles of your arms and shoulders to swing the putter.

> Always try to quiet the little muscles of your hands and use the big muscles of your arms and shoulders to swing the putter.

Chipping

Jimmie thinks that good chipping is the result of a good setup. He recommends that you address the chip in exactly the position you want to be when you actually hit the ball. The ball position should be a little "back" in the stance, opposite your rear ankle. Jimmie likes to use the rear ankle as a marker because ball position can get somewhat confusing if you open the stance. Because the ball is slightly back in the stance, your hands and the handle of the club will be slightly ahead of the ball at address. This position ensures that you'll catch the ball first, not hit behind the ball. He also says that you should have a little more weight on your front foot, as once again this will ensure that the ball will be hit first, not the turf. He suggests that your weight distribution be 70 percent on your front foot and 30 percent on your back foot.

Pitching

According to Jimmie, the pitch shot should be a short version of your normal shot. It's just a miniswing. All of the positions you have in the full swing should be part of the pitch shot. Your weight distribution should be even, 50 percent on each foot at address. He says that you should have a waist-high backswing, though he acknowledges that this will vary somewhat with the length of the shot, and then swing the clubhead down and through the golf ball.

The pitch shot is played with a wedge. Jimmie notes that when you think of the term *wedge* in general, you think of something you squeeze between two other objects, and says that that's what you're trying to do with the wedge—to swing the clubhead down in that space between the ball and the ground. He says to just swing the club down to the ball, then turn your body right through, just as you would with any other stroke in golf. This type of action allows the clubface to act as a ramp, he says, and the ball rides right up it. That action produces the lift.

Jimmie recommends experimenting with some different wedges for the pitch shot, noting that you develop trust in a certain club by experience. He says that the pitching wedge is usually best if you have some room for the ball to run, while the sand wedge, of course, is best if you need some more loft. Jimmie has not had much luck with the lob wedge and feels that very few students will benefit by having one in the bag because you have to swing too hard with it. He says that it's very good on a shot you may rarely have, like an extremely short greenside bunker shot, but, all in all, it's such a specialty club that it may not be worth the time and energy to learn how to use it.

> Jimmie recommends experimenting with some different wedges for the pitch shot, noting that you develop trust in a certain club by experience.

Bunker Shots

Jimmie thinks that a bunker shot is a game within a game, in that it is totally different than any other shot. In most strokes in golf, you're trying to hit down on the ball with your hands leading. In the bunker shot, on the other hand, you're trying to slide the club through the sand. In fact, he says, if anything he feels the clubhead actually passing his hands as it slides through the sand.

Jimmie stresses once again that the setup is so important. The stance should be a little open. Then you should lay the face of the club back so it's as flat as a pancake. According to him, laying the clubface back like that will make the bounce of the wedge more effective and help the club slide through the sand. The more you lay back (or open) the clubface, the more you have to open the stance so that a line across the toes of a right-handed player will point to the left of the target. If you've set the swing up properly, he says, you can hit down on the ball.

When playing a bunker shot, Jimmie advises that you swing really hard because most of the energy will be used to move the sand and force the ball up in the air. He did an experiment with a device that measured clubhead speed and came to the conclusion that you need a clubhead speed of at least 55 miles per hour to produce enough power to get the divot of sand and the ball out of the bunker. The bottom line, as he says, is that you have to swing pretty hard in the greenside bunker to properly play the shot. Good clubhead speed will also produce loft on the shot, which is necessary in those deep sand bunkers. If you don't have enough speed, he says, then you have to hit closer to the ball, and that gets to be dangerous territory. If you generate good speed, then you can swing the club so that it enters the sand well behind the ball. Jimmie says that you need to "get mad at the sand" and give it a ride. You want to take a full-length, relaxed swing and hear the sound the clubhead makes as it glides through the sand. He notes that that kind of "thumping" sound will tell you that the clubhead has bounced or glided through the sand. The sound of the club digging in is not nearly as pleasing, he says, and the results aren't either. You have to commit and be aggressive to be a good bunker player.

> You need a clubhead speed of at least 55 miles per hour to produce enough power to get the divot of sand and the ball out of the bunker.

The Mental Aspect

In all of the shots around the greens, Jimmie recommends that you do the following five things in order. First, assess the situation. Second, analyze the different ways you may play the stroke. Third, make a plan that you are comfortable with, which should be to play the one type of shot you know you can play. Fourth, imagine the shot. And fifth, execute it.

Jimmie notes that everyone has different abilities to be good at the short game; some people just have more of an aptitude for the short game than others. But, he says, everyone can improve. Practice breeds confidence, and you have to trust in your own abilities. You have to commit to your plan and stick with it.

To help with nerves in competition, Jimmie likes to eat light and drink plenty of water. He feels that it's a big burden on your system to try to digest a heavy breakfast when you're already anxious about the first tee shot.

When you do get to the first tee, he says, just trust your game. It takes some experience to really handle tournament pressure. The more you put your game in competition, however, the easier it becomes. (And, he notes, if it's any consolation, everyone else there is nervous, too!) Jimmie advises that you be confident in your abilities and trust your swing.

15

Mary Slinkard

Teaching Professional, Plantation Golf Resort

Putting

When teaching putting, Mary is a big believer in establishing a consistent tempo with the putting stroke. You should swing the putter at an even pace on the backswing and the forward swing. To help establish that tempo, she recommends using a metronome during the putting lessons. As in learning any type of new skill, she notes, whether it be a musical instrument or sport, we all have different aptitudes and learn at different speeds. Mary thinks that the use of the metronome accelerates that learning process.

Some other key points about putting that Mary emphasizes:

Mary Slinkard is the teaching professional at the Plantation Golf Resort in Crystal River, Florida. Mary is one of the best players in her PGA section and was voted one of the Top 50 Women Teachers by *Golf for Women*.

Plantation Golf Resort has been home to the Florida Women's Open. Many of the current LPGA Tour stars had their start in that tournament.

1. Keep your lower body still. The putting stroke does not require a weight shift or any extra movement.
2. Keep your eyes and head still over the ball.
3. Think about the distance you want to roll the ball and the length of your putting stroke. There should be no deceleration in the stroke.
4. Trust your instincts. We are athletes in this sport, and you should trust those athletic instincts.

Chipping

Mary feels that tempo is as important in chipping as in putting. She recommends allowing the clubhead to swing back and forth at an even pace, and notes that the length of the backswing should match the length of the follow-through. To change the distance of the chip shot, she says, you should change the length of the swing and choose different clubs. A chip shot made with a 6 iron, for example, will fly lower, roll more, and go farther than a chip shot made using an 8 iron with the same size swing. Learning to use different clubs around the green is a big step to an improved short game.

> Learning to use different clubs around the green is a big step to an improved short game.

Pitching

Mary recommends that a pitch shot be played with a pitching wedge. She also says, however, that you can use a sand wedge if you need extra loft. Her approach is to address the ball in the middle of the stance, with more of the body weight on the front foot than on the rear foot. This will ensure that the ball is contacted more on the down-swing than on the upswing.

One of Mary's key recommendations on this shot is to keep your head still. She says that there is no need for extra motion here. Also, when you swing, keep your hands moving past the ball—again, to guarantee good contact. A good way that she suggests to make sure your hands are in front of the ball at contact is to finish with a shortened follow-through, leaving the shaft at a vertical angle to the ground. This action is the opposite of "scooping" the ball. After you do that a few times as a drill, Mary then recommends that you swing to a regular finish position.

Mary thinks that poor pitching shots come from slowing down the hands, which allows the clubhead to move past the hands. This results in the clubhead hitting behind the ball or in the clubhead striking the middle of the ball, causing

> Poor pitching shots come from slowing down the hands, which allows the clubhead to move past the hands.

Mary Slinkard emphasizes that the loft of the club will "do the work" to get the ball in the air. Notice that in the follow-through the shaft of the club is still vertical. This simple thought will get those short pitches the required loft every time.

the ball to scurry across the green. Instead, the good swing thought she offers for this shot is "to keep your hands moving."

Lob Shots

According to Mary, the lob shot can be played with either a sand wedge or a 60-degree wedge. If you use the 60-degree wedge, she notes, you won't have to open the stance much or even at all. If you use the sand wedge, however, you will want to open the stance slightly. One of Mary's key points on this shot is to once again keep your hands moving. She emphasizes how similar the impact position is for all golf shots, with the hands ahead of the clubhead at impact.

Bunker Shots

To learn how to hit bunker shots, Mary recommends that you draw a 6-inch box in the sand, with the ball at the center. She says that the beginning of the box is the middle of the stance, which means that the ball is forward in the stance. Mary then says that you should hit the entire box of sand, ball and all, onto the green. She states that this works every time!

Mary has a good method to vary the distance you hit a bunker shot: vary the size and speed of the swing, just as you do with every other shot in golf. For a short sand shot, choke up on the handle a little and make a short swing with a short follow-through. For a long sand shot, hold the handle as you would for a long shot and make a long swing with a long follow-through.

The Mental Aspect

Mary thinks that it's very important to have a good, standard preshot routine. She suggests that you go through the same motions, at the same pace, every time you hit a shot. It is the first step to consistent play. She also recommends that you stand behind the ball so that you can see the intended line of flight. Then visualize the shot, take the grip, address the ball, and swing away with confidence.

If you are having trouble handling pressure, Mary advises you not to stand over the ball too long. She notes that as you stand over the ball, your muscles will tighten. Instead, she says, make a plan and hit it quick when the heat is on.

A Final Thought

Mary has a good exercise to emphasize the importance of the short game. The next time you play, she suggests that you count how many times you took more than three strokes from within 50 yards of the green. With practice, she says, you should be able to get down to three strokes to the pin from this distance. Add those excess strokes up, then deduct them from your score that day. The final total will be a good indicator of what type of golfer you can be.

> Stand behind the ball so that you can see the intended line of flight. Then visualize the shot, take the grip, address the ball, and swing away with confidence.

Ron Philo Sr.

Head of Instruction, Amelia Island Plantation

16

Putting

Ron Sr. has two simple and effective rules to good putting. His first rule is that the ball should be well forward in the stance, almost even with the front foot (the left foot if you are right handed). Having the ball forward allows you to "see" the line of the putt better, because your eyes are behind the ball. He says that if you were to draw a line directly from your eyes downward, that line would be on the line of the putt, but behind the ball. This position is similar to sighting a rifle. Ron notes that Jack Nicklaus used this style and was certainly one of the best putters in all of golf history.

Ron's second rule to good putting is to keep your hands "quiet" during the putting stroke. Your wrists should never hinge. He says that once your putting grip has been established,

Ron Philo Sr. is Head of Instruction at the Amelia Island Plantation in Amelia Island, Florida, just north of Jacksonville. Ron Sr. is a successful player, having won the scoring average in the Northeast New York PGA Section and the Jenny Open, among many other events. Ron has a daughter and a son who are truly great players: Laura Diaz, who has been one of the leading players on the LPGA Tour, and Ron Philo Jr., who is featured in the next chapter.

Amelia Island Plantation is a seventy-two-hole complex on the very northern east coast of Florida. It boasts a great golf course that enjoys four miles of coastline and four miles of untouched marshland.

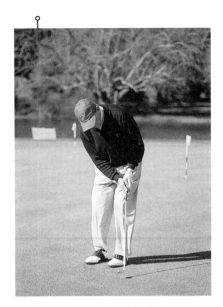

Once you have established the correct address position, swing the putter with your arms and shoulders. Notice that there is no wrist action. This style of putting produces an even and smooth putting stroke, making it very easy to control distance.

your hands do nothing except hold on to the putter. Your wrists stay firm and solid; there is no "breakdown" of the wrists.

According to Ron, you may need to experiment some to find a putting grip that will not break down. One option he suggests is the cross-handed style, which is probably the easiest and most effective way to make a change. To use this grip, have your left hand grip the putter below your right hand (the opposite for left-handers). Simply switch your hands on the handle of the club—the top hand holds the handle where the bottom hand was and the bottom hand holds the handle where the top hand was. This grip prevents that dreaded right-hand flip at the ball and should give you a smoother putting stroke.

Another option Ron suggests is the "Bernhard Langer grip." Bernhard actually holds his club mostly in his left hand, low on the handle. His right hand holds the end of the handle and left forearm. The entire handle of the club is pressed against the forearm so that the right hand can grip both. Ron's point is that you should try anything to prevent your wrist from breaking during the putting stroke.

To make those nerve-wracking 3-foot putts, Ron suggests that you look at the hole, not the ball, as you putt. This puts the focus on the hole. Set the blade squarely behind the ball, he advises, then look at the hole, not at the ball.

Another fact of life that Ron addresses is that vision changes over time. That happens to everyone. You have to be aware that your vision and perceptions may have changed and that adjustments to alignment are natural. What once seemed like the perfect aim and alignment may not be there. So if you find yourself having trouble lining up the putt, have a good professional check your alignment and make any changes necessary.

Pitching

Ron believes that the pitch shot is just a miniswing. This miniswing has all of the characteristics of the full swing, but it's shorter. In the pitch shot, he notes, you really learn how to move your body by transferring weight and using your legs to support the swinging action of the club.

Ron describes the proper sequence of movements in the pitch shot. Your weight transfers to your back foot as you start the swing. There is a slight turn of the shoulders. On the forward swing, your weight transfers to your front foot; the handle of the club moves with the body; and finally there is the follow-through, with your weight on your front foot, your chest facing the target, and your club waist high. Ron feels that this sequence is a wonderful place to practice when you go off your game. The miniswing will give you all of the feedback you need to straighten out your full shots.

Ron's club of choice for all pitch shots is the sand wedge. He finds it to be a very versatile club. If the situation calls for a low shot, Ron suggests that you square your stance and play the ball back in the stance; for a high shot, play the ball forward and open your stance. He feels that you can do anything you'd like with this club—it just takes some experimenting.

He also says that it's better to get very familiar with one club than to have a bag of wedges that may just confuse the issue. Lob wedges in particular may be difficult to play. If the situation calls for more loft, for example, learn to open your stance; Ron feels

> To make those nerve-wracking 3-foot putts, Ron suggests that you look at the hole, not the ball, as you putt.

that it's more reliable to lay back the sand wedge than to use the lob wedge. He feels that you'll be more successful tuning into the feel, the weight, the shaft flex, and the loft of one club than adjusting to the feel of one or two other wedges. It's almost impossible to have wedges that accurately match each other for weight, shaft flex, and feel in general, so Ron suggests that you stick with just the sand wedge.

Ron feels there is no substitute for practicing to acquire a feel for the pitch shot. Don't overanalyze the shot, he says. Take a look at it, take a practice swing to get an idea how much swing to create, and then play. Trust your instincts and your athletic ability. According to Ron, playing short pitches—and actually every short stroke—is an art, not a science. He relies on acquiring a good feel for the shot rather than a mechanical approach.

> You'll be more successful tuning into the feel, the weight, the shaft flex, and the loft of one club than adjusting to the feel of one or two other wedges.

Bunker Shots

Ron says that one of the most important shots to learn is the bunker shot. His approach is the basic slightly "open the stance and open the clubface" style and a "punch it out" technique. During the swing, the clubhead should enter the sand about 2 inches behind the ball and then keep moving to the finish.

He recommends keeping the clubface open throughout the shot, even to the finish position. At the finish, the clubface should be pointing toward the sky. He thinks that it is also important to remember that you have to move your body with the club, just as we did with the pitch shot.

According to Ron, swinging the club through the sand requires some muscle and some speed, so you have to make a basic golf swing. You have to transfer your weight and move your body with the club, the same as a full swing from the fairway with any iron. He feels that this idea of playing the sand shot as a stroke from the fairway validates the golf swing—you need the power of a swing to move both the ball and the sand out of the bunker.

Ron offers a final tip for learning to play bunker shots. He recommends using a magnet attached to a small stick to demonstrate how much loft is required to pop the ball out of the bunker. If you allow the sand wedge to lie naturally on the ground and then put the magnet on the clubface, the stick will point upward, showing the amount of loft the clubface will produce.

The Mental Aspect

Ron has a good approach to the mental side of the game. He recommends that you not dwell on the poor shots and worry about what happened. Get away from overanalyzing, as he finds that it is too negative and self-defeating. Instead, he says, reflect on the good shots, remembering the feel of them and the positive approach you had before the stroke. Reflecting on the dos and not the don'ts will keep you in a positive and aggressive state of mind. He suggests that the ultimate don't is nothing at all, so, in his words, "think positive, good things will result."

> Reflect on the good shots, remembering the feel of them and the positive approach you had before the stroke.

Ron Philo Jr.

Head Professional, Metropolis Country Club

Putting

Ron Jr. thinks that the setup and your posture are very important components of putting. He recommends that the ball be forward in your stance so that your eyes are behind the ball at address. This way your eyes are on the line of the putt, just a few inches behind the ball, so that you can easily see the line when you address the ball.

Another suggestion that Ron Jr. offers is to match the action of your right hand (or left, for left-handers) with the face of the putter. Thus, the right hand and the putter blade should be square to the hole at address. When you swing through the right hand, your right arm and the putter blade will go directly toward the target.

Finally, when putting, Ron Jr. feels that it's very important to focus on where you want the

Ron Philo Jr. is the head professional at Metropolis Country Club in White Plains, New York. He has played competitively at the highest levels, including one U.S. Open and six PGA Championships, and has won the New England Open, the New England PGA, the Metropolitan PGA, the Rhode Island Open, and the National Club Pro Championship—the most coveted of tournaments for club professionals. His father, Ron Philo Sr., was featured in the previous chapter.

Metropolis is one of the finest clubs in the New York metropolitan area. Ron follows three golfing legends at Metropolis as the head professional: Paul Runyan, "Lighthorse" Harry Cooper, and Gene Borek.

ball to go. He recommends that you imagine the putt before you actually hit it. On very short putts, Ron Jr. says that you should not look at the ball, but instead look into the hole. This takes your mind off of the ball. He says that you need to trust that you are properly aligned, look into the hole, and then make a smooth stroke.

Chipping

Ron Jr. thinks that visualization is the key to making chip shots. The first step is to try to picture what the shot should look like, in other words, how much airtime and how much roll the ball will have. The next step is to choose the correct plan to match the flight that you've envisioned. If you "see" a low running chip shot, he says that you may want to choose a 4, a 5, or a 6 iron. If, on the other hand, you are looking for a more lofted chip, you will want to choose a 7, an 8, or a 9 iron or a pitching wedge for the shot.

Pitching

In a pitch shot, you are trying to loft the ball, so Ron Jr. suggests that you use a sand wedge or a lob wedge. To keep the swing fairly short, he recommends that your feet be close together, which will help you feel the length of the swing. At address, he says, there should be a little more weight on your front foot than on your back foot. This setup puts your body ahead of the ball, which ensures that you'll hit the ball cleanly and with a slight descending angle.

The swing in the pitch shot is a miniswing. Ron Jr. advises that you keep your left arm long on the backswing. This concept is particularly helpful if you have a tendency to lift rather than to swing the club. He notes that the swinging action will help the clubhead maintain a shallower path. The shallower path will be much more consistent than one that comes up too quickly. If the club comes up quickly, he notes, it will be swung down too steeply on the downswing and the sharp angle will create poor contact. The clubhead will either strike the ground before the ball so that you hit a "fat" shot or come down more on top of the ball so that you hit a "thin" shot. On the forward swing, Ron Jr. suggests that you swing your right arm and hand through to the hole. Your right arm should swing past your left knee (reversed, of course, for left-handers).

As his final tip about pitching, Ron Jr. is very emphatic about focusing solely on the target and not on the ball in a pitch shot. He says that you need to concentrate on where you want the ball to go.

> Ron Jr. is very emphatic about focusing solely on the target and not on the ball in a pitch shot. He says that you need to concentrate on where you want the ball to go.

Bunker Shots

In teaching the bunker shot, the first step Ron Jr. suggests is to dig your feet slightly into the sand bunker at address. He finds that this digging in does two things. First, it gives you a feel for the sand in that particular bunker. He notes that often the top layer of sand in a bunker looks white and soft, and only after you swing the club do you find that there is a layer of firm sand or even clay just below. Second, digging in slightly will provide you with more stable footing. After all, he reminds us, it takes some energy to move the sand and the ball out of the bunker, so you have to make a fairly full swing. A sure-footed stance will make that swing easier.

Ron Jr. offers two tips for hitting the ball in the bunker. First, he cautions that you shouldn't be afraid to hit into the sand. You have

One of the keys to good sand play around the greens is an aggressive swing. Notice that the player has a full finish.

to commit to the sand shot. And second, he says, hit "through" the sand, as he finds that the sand shot requires a full follow-through.

Focusing

Ron Jr. offers a few ways to improve your focus in the short game. One is to think about where you want the ball to go. Look at the target and take your practice swing with the target in mind. He reminds us that so often we just look at the ball and forget where we would like it to go. Another way to improve focus, Ron Jr. finds, is to put yourself in trouble spots where you have to be creative, such as a place where you have to hit the ball through a narrow opening or over a bush. This exercise makes you rely on your imagination, picture the shot, and forget about the ball.

Handling Pressure

Ron Jr. wants to remind you that pressure comes from your imagination. And as you create it, you can also make it disappear. If you are like most golfers, you see the pressure as a train or some other type of problem running toward you. Ron suggests that you instead picture that pressure running in the opposite direction, away from you. He notes that that pressure may take a specific form or it may just be the feeling that the pressure is flowing in the other direction, but the point is to send it away.

Another way that Ron Jr. suggests to address any type of pressure on the golf course is to remind yourself how much you enjoy this great game and how much you enjoy the course and your friends. And finally, rather than worrying about failure, he recommends that you think the opposite. Picture yourself winning that tournament and holding the trophy high or just collecting a Nassau bet. The point, Ron Jr. says, is to think that good things will happen—and they probably will.

Another way to improve focus, Ron Jr. finds, is to put yourself in trouble spots where you have to be creative, such as a place where you have to hit the ball through a narrow opening or over a bush.

18

Mary Lou Mulfur

Head Coach of Women's Golf,
University of Washington

Putting

Mary Lou thinks that the putting is about feel and not about mechanics. She says that once you have achieved some good fundamentals as to the correct grip and stance for putting, you should rely on your athletic ability.

Mary Lou also recommends that you try to see the putt before you hit it. Create a visual in your mind. Try to picture how it will "break" and what speed you expect the ball to roll. Mary Lou feels that too much emphasis is placed on the mechanics of the putting stroke and not enough on creating a good picture. Instead, go ahead and execute it without a lot of detail or overanalysis.

Mary Lou Mulfur is head coach of the women's golf team at the University of Washington. Mary Lou was the PAC-10 Coach of the Year twice, once in 1988 and then again in 1999. She is also a fine player herself, having played in two U.S. Opens and three U.S. Amateurs.

The home course for the University of Washington is Washington National, which was the site of the 2002 NCAA Women's Championship and the 2003 NCAA Men's Regional Championship as well as the host of the 2006 NCAA Women's West Regional Championship.

Chipping

For chip shots, Mary Lou suggests that you get the ball on the ground as quickly as possible. She feels that you should hit the simplest shot, which in almost all cases is a chip shot played with a middle iron (a 4 to a 7 iron). She has two rules to go by when chipping. First, land the ball on the green. If possible, you should avoid running it up through the fringe or apron. Second, get the ball running as soon as possible. This running technique will resemble a putt, which she notes is one shot in golf everyone can play with some success. Getting the ball running will also make it more likely that you'll reach the hole. If you play a lofted shot, she says, there is a very good chance that you'll end up short of the hole. And a third advantage of running the ball up is that even if you don't contact the ball solidly, there is still a good possibility that the ball will roll up fairly close to the hole. Mary Lou feels that the mistakes and not perfectly played shots just work out better with the running technique when chipping.

> She has two rules to go by when chipping. First, land the ball on the green. Second, get the ball running as soon as possible.

Bunker Shots

Mary Lou reminds you that, for playing a bunker shot, the sand wedge was designed to slide through the sand, so you don't have to make any of the stance adjustments that so many teachers recommend. Rather than making those adjustments, she says, address the ball with a square stance; position the ball slightly forward in your stance; look at the area behind the ball, about 2 inches behind; and then swing away. She notes that the sand wedge has more metal on the bottom or sole of the club than the other irons; that difference in design allows the wedge to slide rather than dig into the sand. Ultimately, according to Mary Lou, you should play the sand shot as though you were playing from the fairway.

Practicing

Mary Lou thinks that it's important to know how far each one of your clubs, especially wedges, hits the ball. Many golfers today carry three or four wedges. If you have time to practice with this many wedges, Mary Lou finds that you can develop a good assortment of different types of shots. The first step in that development is to know how far each wedge will go with a full and then a half swing. She recommends finding a level fairway or practice area, hitting your wedges with a full and then a miniswing, and walking off the distances. That will give you a sense of what club is the best one to choose on the course.

Mary Lou has another suggestion for positive practice sessions, which is to keep your practice competitive by either practicing with a friend or creating games yourself. She recommends moving from one situation to the next to see how you do playing against your friend or against your own personal best. Try to keep it "real" by using only one ball and moving from one situation to the next. She notes that so often we put down a pile of balls and just keep swinging away, creating a pretty boring and unproductive practice session, so she encourages you to vary the putts, chips, and pitches. That will make practice a lot more fun and real.

She recommends finding a level fairway or practice area, hitting your wedges with a full and then a miniswing, and walking off the distances.

The Mental Aspect

Mary Lou feels that golf is essentially a simple game. You are just trying to hit the ball from point A to point B, so, she says, don't make it more complicated than that. She finds that pressure of any sort, in tournaments or even in a match against friends, can be your friend. Embrace it, she says, and use it to help you focus better. According to Mary Lou, the bottom line is that golf is a game, so you should play it and not get tangled up in technical mechanics. Just move that white ball from A to B as simply as possible.

19

Shawn Baker

Head Professional, The Greens at Half Hollow

Putting

Shawn teaches that you should rely on the weight of the putter to move the ball. There is no striking or hitting action but instead a smooth putting stroke. The ball just gets in the way of the putter as it swings toward the hole. He thinks that the length of the stroke should increase with the length of the putt. As the putt gets longer, however, you should rely on the smooth stroking action of the putter and not try to hit the ball harder. According to Shawn, any "hit" impulse you feel when putting will make it difficult to feel the distance. He also says that this idea of a smooth stroke and not a hit will also give you the feeling of rolling the ball. The roll of the ball will be true and the ball will not bounce on the way to the hole.

Shawn Baker is the head professional at the The Greens at Half Hollow in Melville, New York. Shawn has been a premier player in both the New England and Metropolitan PGA sections, winning the Assistant Professional of the Year Award in the Metropolitan Section. Shawn also had an incredible amateur career before becoming a golf professional. He won the Northeast Amateur once and the Vermont Amateur five times.

The Greens at Half Hallow is a challenging par 60 course, five minutes from the Bethpage golf complex. The course has hosted several Metropolitan PGA Junior events.

> Any "hit" impulse you feel when putting will make it difficult to feel the distance.

Shawn believes that putting is more art than science. If it was science, he says, we'd all play the same way. Putting requires both feel and adjusting to different circumstances, such as wind, grass length, slopes, and many other factors. So, he says, don't try to putt like someone else; instead, he suggests that you find a style that feels comfortable to you and stick with it. There are a variety of ways to roll the ball on the green. Keep experimenting with different putting grips, stances, and strokes until you find a feel that you can trust.

Shawn notes that few players line the putter up squarely and perfectly to the hole. One part of lining up the shot properly is where you position the ball relative to the address position. If you play the ball too far forward in the stance, he says, there is a good chance that you will have the putter blade aimed to the left. If the ball is positioned too far back in the stance, however, there is a good chance that the putter blade will be aimed to the right. Thus, he thinks that ball position relative to the stance is a key ingredient in proper alignment.

Chipping and Pitching

Shawn feels that, in chip shots and pitch shots, as in all golf shots, all we're ever really trying to do is hit the ball solidly. To do this, he suggests that you position the ball slightly back in the stance and have more weight on your front foot. This will produce a more descending action. Another point he makes is to let your club swing, not to steer it. Many golfers hold on to the club too tightly and try to force the clubhead directly down the line. In the correct action, Shawn believes, the shaft of the club does not go at the target but exits to the left (for right-handed players). The swing on the short shots is the same as the swing on the full swing, and so the head of the club goes toward the target and then comes back to the inside after the ball has been struck.

Shawn has a good thought for all shots around the green and that is to keep your arms moving. He notes that most mishits occur when you quit on the shot, so the simple technique of keeping your arms moving will get you through the ball and provide the necessary follow-through.

A good thought around the greens is to keep your arms moving.

Bunker Shots

Shawn finds that sand bunkers are the most mentally challenging part of the game. Shawn notes that even the greatest players have at one time or another sailed one over the green from the bunker. He says, however, that this common memory must be overcome, because if you have the constant fear that you will hit the dreaded shot that goes over the green, you will never commit to the fairly full swing that is required to execute this shot properly.

Shawn's basic strategy for bunker shots is to open the stance, lay the face of the sand wedge back, aim about 2 inches behind the ball, take a divot of sand out of the bunker, and then follow through. If the ball is anywhere in that divot of sand, the ball and divot will both come out and land on the green. As he says, the mechanics are not difficult. Rather, it is the fear of the ball sailing over the green that must be conquered. Confidence is required, and he finds that the two ingredients to achieve confidence are knowledge and practice. While he realizes that there are not many places to practice bunker play, he suggests that if you can find a decent practice bunker, you should invest some time there. It won't be long before you develop confidence, and what was once your worst shot may become your best.

20

Ken Morton Sr.

Head Professional, Haggin Oaks Golf Complex

Putting

Ken believes that the game of golf works from the hole out. Putting is how he coaches people to make solid contact, how to aim and to judge distances. Putting is a great way to start coaching golf, by educating the student to read the break of the greens.

Ken has had success with many students who have had the "yips," a quick, jerky, out-of-control movement that happens when you are trying to make a smooth stroke, or other cases of just bad putting. He has found that most of these players are either very afraid that they are going to miss the putt or are people who have trouble focusing in general.

From Ken's point of view, making 3-foot putts is all about visualization and relaxation, and possibly even breathing. He finds that the

Ken Morton Sr. is in his forty-eighth year at Haggin Oaks Golf Complex in Sacramento, California. He has won about every national award the PGA of America has to give out. The list includes the 2001 PGA Junior Golf Leader Award, the 1998 and 1991 Merchandiser of the Year Award, the 1996 National PGA Horton Smith Award, as well as the coveted 1998 PGA Golf Professional of the Year Award. Ken is also a Master PGA Professional and was inducted into the PGA Hall of Fame in 2005.

The Haggin Oaks Golf Complex is a thirty-six-hole municipal facility that was originally designed by the famous Alister MacKenzie.

best system to overcome the yips is to make sure that you can visualize the break of the putt and the pace at which the ball needs to be rolled to achieve that break. Ken strongly encourages you to make sure you can see what the putt does in your mind and then to close your eyes and practice your stroke until your practice stroke matches the roll of the ball. Then you should get up to the putt with your regular routine. When you are ready to stroke the putt, Ken says you should close your eyes, try to visualize the same stroke you used without the ball, and then hit it with your eyes open. Ken feels that this process has overcome nine out of ten cases of the yips.

Chipping and Pitching

Ken feels that the chip shot is both the miniversion and the starting point of the full swing. This is where he teaches to visualize how the ball is actually struck. Once you understand how the ball gets airborne, he says, the learning curve for the full shots is considerably shortened. This is also where Ken introduces the basics of posture, grip, stance, and balance. Using the standard grip for the full shot, Ken relates the size of the swing to the distance of the shot. For a 30-foot chip, Ken demonstrates that the ball should fly less than a third of the distance in the air and then roll the rest of the way. The size of the swing may have a backswing of only 1 foot and a follow-through of 1 foot. As Ken moves to a 60-foot chip, the size of the back and forward swings increase. Increasing the length of the swing to accommodate a longer shot gives you a feel for graduating to the full swing.

Ken says that you can see that the short pitch has all the qualities of a good swing. Learning the fundamentals here best prepares you for fuller swings. He notes that if you can't do what you should do on a short chip, the problem will only magnify as your swing grows.

Ken says that the pitch shot is where your swing begins to grow. He still emphasizes that how the ball is struck is important, but he also adds more instruction on shifting your weight and setting and resetting your wrist to prepare for techniques associated with the full swing. The size of the swing will also increase when more distance is required. For a short pitch the clubhead should be swung about knee high to knee high, for a medium length pitch the clubhead should be swung waist high to waist high, and for a long pitch the clubhead should be swung almost shoulder high to shoulder high. The length of the pitch shot is now approaching a full swing. Ken believes mastering the pitch shot and increasing the length of the swing is the best way to develop a good, full, repeating golf swing.

Ken Morton Sr. builds the swing around the medium-distance (about a 50-yard) pitch shot. With this shot, you can develop all of the basics: a good grip, proper posture, good balance, and the feel of transferring your weight.

Bunker Shots

Bunker shots are where Ken coaches how the bottom of the club works and how to use the sand to do much of the work for you, using the fried egg theory. To demonstrate, Ken draws a circle 2 to 3 inches around the ball in the sand and explains that the circle outside the ball is the white of the egg and the ball is the yellow in the frying pan. The secret of the good bunker shot, he says, is to

> It is very important to stay over the ball, meaning that there should be no sway in your swing.

hit the entire egg out of the bunker without breaking the yoke.

Ken teaches that it is very important to stay over the ball, meaning that there should be no sway in your swing. He also says that if you learn how to use the sole of the club, a small mistake won't mean disaster. When you are using the sole correctly, it will slide through the sand. If the club enters the sand 1 to 3 inches behind the ball, the ball will come out of the bunker and produce a satisfactory result.

Lob Shots

When teaching lob shots, Ken wants you to understand how ball position and clubface position at impact affect the ball's flight, back spin, and roll. The ball positioned slightly forward in the stance and the clubface laid slightly back will produce maximum height on this shot.

The lob is also a shot for which Ken stresses the importance of being relaxed and acquiring a feel for the pace of the swing. He explains that the outcome is usually bad when the shot is rushed. He also takes this time to emphasize the importance of the preshot routine so that you can achieve a consistent pace and rhythm.

A Teaching Trick That Works on the Short Game

Ken teaches tricks and shortcuts for the short game. He uses these tricks to speed up the learning process so that you can make changes through feel as well as through instruction. After years of teaching, Ken finds that most problems occur from improper balance or from too much tension. The following is Ken's favorite teaching aid to help you understand the appropriate grip pressure. First, grip the club as hard as you can and register what that feels like. Next, grip the club so lightly that the club easily twists in your hands. Then, on a scale of one to ten (with ten being as hard as you can grip the club), grip the club at a two or three level. At this point, he asks why you're doing this drill. From this exercise, you can realize that only through soft grip pressure can you achieve the correct wrist action and flexibility required to produce speed in the swing. After you monitor this pressure for a while, Ken says, it is amazing the changes that can happen.

The Mental Aspect

Ken strongly believes that the mental side of golf is about educating yourself how to think. He notes that the world today bombards all of us with mostly negative news and that many people learn to think with fear in negative (can't do) terms instead in positive (can do) terms. Ken sees himself as a coach and his task as pulling out of you how you think and how you feel about what you are trying to accomplish, and then asking you to hit a shot. As you hit more balls, he then reeducates you in several ways on how to think appropriately and then consistently asks you how you are thinking until the answer and the results are consistently correct. When you are practicing at home, he encourages you to continually check in with yourself about what you are thinking and how it is affecting your shots. Bad golf usually means bad thinking. Good golf usually means good thinking.

> Bad golf usually means bad thinking. Good golf usually means good thinking.

21

Mark Aebli

Teaching Professional, The Original Golf School at
Plantation Golf Resort

Putting

Mark's first goal when teaching putting is to find a technique by which you can produce a solid hit by the putter. This technique may be to have your eyes directly over or to have them slightly inside the line of the putt at the address position. To decide this, you will need to determine your dominant eye, which is the one responsible for "sighting." Mark notes that you look down the line of the putt with your dominant eye the same way as you would look down the barrel of a gun to sight it. If you are a left-eye dominant player, Mark says, the ball should be forward in the stance. Your eyes should still be over the line of the putt but several inches behind the ball. If you are a right-eye dominant player, the ball should be more centered in the stance. You can still see the

Mark Aebli is a teaching professional at The Original Golf School at Plantation Golf Resort in Crystal River, Florida, and at Mount Snow Golf Club in West Dover, Vermont. Mark was voted the number one teacher in the state of Vermont by *Golf Digest*. As a competitor, Mark won three times on the Asian Tour and once on the South American Tour. His biggest win was the Hong Kong Open, when he beat Greg Norman down the stretch when Norman was rated the number one player in the world.

Mount Snow Golf Club is a beautiful championship course located in the Green Mountains of Southern Vermont. It has hosted the New England Open, The New England PGA Championship, and the Vermont Senior Open.

line as you look toward the hole. Thus, if you are a right-handed golfer and you are left-eye dominant, you should address the putt with your eyes behind the ball. Mark's best example of this type of setup is Jack Nicklaus—his eyes are directly over the line but behind the ball.

Mark's method to determine the dominant eye is to have you point at a ball on the green with your index finger. Close one eye and open it, then close the other eye and open it. With one eye open, the ball will stay in the same place; with the other eye open, the ball will appear to move. The eye that sees the ball in the same place is the dominant eye. If you can't "sight it" with your master eye, Mark says, you won't ever be able to get the ball on line.

According to Mark, speed is very important in putting, and the ability to control speed takes practice. To help you get a better idea of speed, he suggests that you walk off the putt to figure out how many paces the putt is. While this is not a surefire method to hit the putt the correct distance, it does serve the purpose of getting you in the ballpark, distance-wise. In most putts of three paces, for example, the size of the stroke will be about 6 inches forward and back. For a putt of ten paces, the size of the stroke will be about 18 inches forward and back. We are all different and there are countless variables, Mark says, but matching the paces to the size of the stroke is a good place to start. He notes that this can be done quickly, even before it's your turn to putt, and should not in any way slow down play.

Chipping

In the chip shot, Mark teaches that you should have a little more weight on the front foot at address, approximately 60 percent on

> If you can't "sight it" with your master eye, Mark says, you won't ever be able to get the ball on line.

the front foot and 40 percent on the back foot. And once again, he says, the dominant eye theory is important. If your left eye is the dominant eye, the ball should not be back in the stance. The correct ball position for those with a dominant left eye should be center to slightly forward. For those with a dominant right eye, the ball should be slightly back of center. Swing the club with a smooth shoulder motion with very little wrist break. This motion will produce a true roll for the ball.

Mark teaches that your grip pressure should be soft if the ball is sitting well in the grass and that you should then use a sweeping motion. If the ball is sitting down in the grass, he suggests that you use a firmer grip. The firmer grip will produce a little more downward pressure and loft the ball from the turf.

Mark thinks that club selection for the chip shot should be somewhere between the 7 iron and the lob wedge and that it's a good idea to become familiar with all of the lofted short irons in your bag. The changes in equipment in recent years have made him change his approach somewhat in club selection. From his perspective, reduced lofts in most irons and the harder golf balls require chipping with more lofted clubs now than in the past.

Pitching

Mark teaches that the single most important concept in the pitch shot is to hit it on the "downbeat." This means that the club must be descending if the ball is going to achieve the proper trajectory and loft. The feeling in the pitch shot is that you're going to press the ball into the turf. At contact, he says, your

> Mark teaches that the single most important concept in the pitch shot is to hit it on the "downbeat." This means that the club must be descending if the ball is going to achieve the proper trajectory and loft.

hands should be slightly ahead of the head of the club, producing a downward action. The downward action and the loft of the club will lift the ball into the air. The best club to pitch with, day in and day out, he says, is the sand wedge because it is the most versatile. If you have time, Mark feels it's a good idea to practice with all your short irons so that you have a wide variety of options around the greens.

Lob Shots

Mark notes that there can be a big difference among lofted wedges. If the course you play has a lot of firm turf around the green, he says, you would want to play a wedge that has a lot of loft but not a lot of bounce. (Bounce is measured by the shape and size of the sole of the club. If the sole of the club is wide and designed at a certain angle it will not dig into the turf but will slide.) Mark suggests that when you purchase a lob wedge, you get some professional help to make sure that the particular wedge fits the situations you commonly experience at your home course or in your area. He finds that a 60-degree wedge with a 4- to 6-degree bounce usually suits most courses and situations.

Mark thinks that to play lob shots or use a 60-degree wedge with proficiency, you have to practice, and practice a lot.

Bunker Shots

When you play bunker shots, Mark thinks that you should open the stance slightly. In the address position, he recommends not fully extending your arms, instead preferring that you have just a slight bend in your elbows. He notes that you might feel a little too close to the ball, but says that when you swing the club, your arms will become more extended and you'll swing the club into the sand behind the ball. According to Mark, most players "line drive" the ball out of the bunker because they start with their arms too extended at address. If you start with your arms slightly bent, however, there is a better chance that the club will enter the sand behind the ball.

Mark notes that both Sam Snead and Johnny Revolta said that you cannot use the traditional sand shot approach over 35 yards. So if you have one of those "in-between long bunker shots," he suggests that you try using an 8 or a 9 iron. Open the stance, he says, lay the club back a little, and have the club enter the sand about 2 inches behind the ball. The ball will come out of the sand somewhat lower than with a traditional bunker shot and will run a little. It will normally go about 50 to 60 yards.

Course Management

Mark goes by the old adage "know thyself." By that, he means that you have to know what swing tendencies you have on the course, and you only acquire that knowledge by playing. You have to play a lot of golf, he says, put your game under some pressure, and see how you react. For instance, over time you may find that when you are under pressure you hit the ball to the right. The next time your game gets under pressure, he says, you should figure out a way to prevent the ball from going right and then figure out a way to hit the ball straight. Mark feels that you can't protect against the tendencies in your game if you haven't ana-

The natural force of the swing extends Mark's arms slightly. Beginning with your arms slightly bent ensures that the club enters the sand before the ball and lessens the chance of hitting the ball first and thus over the green.

lyzed your history. What did you do the last time you were under pressure? And how can you make sure that it doesn't happen again? It means paying attention to detail.

Handling Pressure

When you play, Mark encourages you to keep a good sense of humor. After all, it is just golf, and everyone knows that the best in the world sometimes have difficulties. Mark notes that even Tiger Woods seems to laugh at himself when he hits an uncharacteristically errant shot. If you're too tight and take the game too seriously, Mark says, you are doomed to failure. Instead, he recommends that we should all laugh at ourselves—it's the only way to survive and have fun in this most impossible of games.

22

Jim Brotherton

Director of Golf, Old Overton Club

Jim Brotherton is the Director of Golf at Old Overton Club in Birmingham, Alabama. Jim has been very active in the PGA for thirty years and has served on virtually all of the national PGA committees. He was voted National PGA Professional in 2003 and was inducted into the PGA Hall of Fame in 2005.

Old Overton Club was named the Best Private New Club in 1994. It hosts the Jerry Pate National Intercollegiate and The David Toms International each year.

Putting

Jim teaches putting by first covering the proper alignment. Without correct alignment, he says, all else is lost. He then works on grip, stance, and posture. Once you get through those fundamentals, Jim works mostly on the attitude or approach you should have.

According to Jim, players often get confused by getting the feel for the break of the green. The break in the green sometimes provides too much information, and you can start to think too much. Jim tries to simplify this by illustrating that every putt is really a straight putt, it just may be to a different target. If the putt breaks 2 feet to the left, for example, Jim suggests that you aim at a spot 2 feet to the right of the hole. This approach simplifies the process.

> Every putt is really a straight putt, it just may be to a different target. If the putt breaks 2 feet to the left, for example, Jim suggests that you aim at a spot 2 feet to the right of the hole.

Jim teaches a very uncomplicated putting stroke. Swing the putter straight back and straight through. Believe in this approach and convince yourself that it really is that simple, he says, and you can't miss. He emphasizes that rolling the ball with enough speed to easily reach and slightly go by the hole is imperative to becoming a good putter. Aside from the obvious point that a putt left short can't go in, Jim notes that another reason to hit the ball with sufficient speed is that it is much easier to make a 2-foot putt coming from behind the hole than it is dealing with leaving putts left short, right in the heart of the hole (especially if it's for a birdie!).

To improve on short putts, Jim recommends playing "beat the clock" at the end of a putting session. To do this, putt three balls 3 feet from the hole. Do this around the hole four times, at what would be twelve, three, six, and nine o'clock if you could imprint the face of a clock on the green. Make three straight in each direction before you leave the practice green. When you miss, you start over. Jim's thought about this game is that creates just enough pressure to get your attention. He notes that when you are on the course, you may have a 30-footer on the first hole. While you shouldn't expect to make it, you should be able to putt the ball to within 3 feet of the hole, and that's an easy distance to finish because you just made a million of the same length putts at your putting session.

Chipping and Pitching

One of the main shots that Jim teaches is a soft 56-, 58-, or 60-degree wedge from about 5 yards off the green to a close pin, one where there's not much green to work with. Jim teaches a shot with no wrist break, which makes the ball fly softly and roll very little. To produce this shot, he recommends either taping your wrists together or placing an extended shaft under your front arm so that when you swing it is impossible for your wrists to hinge at all. Jim's advice around the greens is to keep the clubhead moving to a follow-through. He says that most poor shots around the green are a result of stopping the clubhead during the swing. Many players stop swinging at the ball once it has been struck because they think that the shot is over. To illustrate how important the follow-through is, Jim uses the example of a 100-meter dash—would you stop at the 50-meter line in a 100-meter dash? Of course not. Likewise, he says, you have to finish the swing to complete your shot.

Handling Pressure

Jim tries to keep golf simple. He teaches that the swing has two parts: (1) a start and (2) a finish. He notes that it's easy to start the swing, so then all of your concentration can be devoted to the finish. According to Jim, there is no need to worry about the middle of the swing, because the entire swing lasts less than two seconds. Jim says that this approach seems to work because every time you make a good finish, you get a good shot!

> Every time you make a good finish, you get a good shot!

23

Bill McDonough

Former Director, The Original Golf School at
Greenview Cove

Putting

As a player and a teacher, Bill has acquired
quite a few tricks along the way. The first tip
he relates about putting is one he learned from
Bobby Brue, one of the real journeymen in
professional golf. Bill says that he was putting
horribly on the Senior Tour for a few weeks.
He went to the practice green where Bobby
Brue happened to be putting. Bill looked at
Bobby's putter and said, "What the heck is that
pink color on the face of your putter?" Bobby
just laughed and said, "Come here, rookie."
Bill took the putter and set it behind the ball.
Bobby asked him, "What do you see?" Bill
said, "I see pink, you dummy!" Bobby said,
"Aha! Move your hands forward until you
don't see pink any more." Essentially, Bobby
was setting his hands to the same starting posi-

> Bill McDonough is the former
> Director of The Original Golf
> School at Greenview Cove
> Country Club in West Palm
> Beach, Florida. Before turning
> professional, Bill won twenty-
> eight prestigious amateur
> tournaments. As a profes-
> sional, Bill qualified for the
> Senior PGA Tour, no small feat
> when only eight players out of
> twenty-five hundred qualify.
> On the Senior Tour, Bill posted
> four top 10 and five top 20
> finishes.

Line up the putt with

the line on the top or

back of the putter.

tion every time. Bill says that he has been doing that ever since.

To help make short putts, Bill received a great tip from Lee Trevino: line up the putt with the line on the top or back of the putter. Bill notes that most golfers try to aim the face of the putter at the hole, but the face of the putter can lie—it may just be off by a fraction. The line on the top of the blade cannot lie, he says, so use it to line up your shot.

Bill offers another trick on short putts. He notes that the width of the putter is just about the width of the hole. On putts under 6 feet that have some break, he recommends aiming the line of the putter at the middle of the hole and then addressing the ball "off center" to allow for the break. If the putt breaks slightly right to left, for example, he says to address the ball on the right side of the line on the putter. If it breaks left to right, you should position the ball on the left side of the line. If you can aim the line, he says, you can do this.

Chipping

Another technique that Bill learned on the Senior Tour applies to chipping. While this tip is a little tricky and applies best to advanced golfers, he notes that all golfers get in this spot. In fact, it's Bill's favorite shot around the green because it's "choke proof." He says that anyone can chip around the green with a 7 or an 8 iron if the grass is short, but what happens when your ball lands in the heavy grass around the green? If you are chipping from the heavy grass, Bill suggests the following: use a sand wedge; address the ball so that it is positioned well back in the stance, opposite your back foot; weaken your grip so that the "V" of your top hand points to your chin; make sure your hands are over your left knee; then swing your club. Bill realizes that this may sound confusing but assures you that it's worth rereading a few times. He promises that the ball will pop out of the lie every time and will run quite a bit. After a little experience with this shot, Bill thinks that you'll get a good feel as to where to land the ball on the green.

Bill feels that looking up before actually hitting the ball is a problem that almost all golfers have. He calls it "anticipating results" before they happen. He offers a good cure for lifting up your head on short shots around the green: hit the ball and keep your head stationary until you hear the ball land on the green. In other words, he says, "don't peek."

A good habit to develop and one that ensures solid contact on short shots is to keep your head stationary until after the ball has been struck. A good trick is to wait until you hear the ball hit the green before you look at the results.

Handling Pressure

Bill notes that everyone gets nervous. The best way to handle pressure, he finds, is to keep it simple. A pressure situation often will get you flustered, so that is the time to go back to the swing thoughts that were successful. You have achieved some success with certain swing keys. To handle pressure, Bill says to ignore the distractions, rely on your swing keys, and give it a ride.

To handle pressure,

Bill says to ignore

the distractions, rely

on your swing keys,

and give it a ride.

24

Bob Affelder

Director, The Original Golf School at Ocean City

Bob Affelder is the Director of The Original Golf School at Ocean City, Maryland. Bob's many victories include the New Hampshire PGA and the Southern Vermont Open.

The courses that host The Original Golf School in Ocean City are the Beach Club and The Links at Lighthouse Sound. The Links at Lighthouse Sound has been called the "Pebble Beach" of the east and was voted among the top ten Best New Public Golf Facility in America by *Golf Magazine*.

Putting

When you are learning to putt, Bob feels that you really need a good preshot routine. Do the same thing every time. He says that you can invent your routine or ask a good teaching professional to help you out. But, he notes, a good routine will get you into a groove and make life easier under pressure.

There are three key points to putting, according to Bob. First, he suggests that you find a putter that you like. He says that there are three clubs in your bag that should be your favorites: the driver, the sand wedge, and the putter. Find a putter with the right weight and "look" for your eye. Second, he recommends developing a stroke that doesn't break down—by that, he means that your wrists don't hinge at all during the putting

> A good routine will get you into a groove and make life easier under pressure.

stroke. (Bob says that it is the claw grip that keeps his wrists steady.) And third, find a stance and style that is comfortable for you.

Bob teaches that in a good putting stance, your eyes should easily be able to see the line of the putt. From this point on, he says, it's repetition—make your routine consistent. Read the putt, select the line, aim the centerline of the putter on the break or the line you want the ball to roll, and think speed. Bob says that his students have had great success with this approach, and he notes that the great putters of the game seem to share these same traits. Whether it's Jack Nicklaus, Tiger Woods, Brad Faxon, or Ben Crenshaw, he says, you know who's putting because of their unique style, which they never change. Bob feels that the more variables you eliminate before you putt, the more simple things become and the more you can rely on your natural instincts.

For short putts, Bob suggests making a positive read of the break. You may have to look at the putt from several angles before you are sure of the break. After you are sure of the break, then you can proceed with confidence. According to Bob, you should trust your read of the putt, aim the centerline of the putter to that line, and concentrate solely on the speed to knock the ball into the back of the cup.

> Trust your read of the putt, aim the centerline of the putter to that line, and concentrate solely on the speed to knock the ball into the back of the cup.

Chipping

Bob feels that the chip shot is not much different than a putt except that you use a lofted club. The chip shot can be played with a number of clubs, ranging from a 5 iron to a wedge. In Bob's opinion, the average golfer tends to limit club selection to one club—usually the most difficult one to play, the wedge. As a result, he says, the chip becomes too complicated, requiring great feel to judge the size swing necessary to carry the ball varying distances in the air.

Bob teaches instead that the idea of the chip is to land the ball on the green and then run it to the hole. He suggests that you use a club without too much loft, which will produce the least amount of airtime and maximum amount of roll. Then, he says, you can shorten the chipping stroke and make it more consistent. His technique is simple: take a narrow stance, position the ball slightly back of center, and stand as close to the ball as if you were putting it. Then make a putting stroke with little wrist action. If the ball is sitting down in the grass, he says that you should use a more lofted club and place extra weight on your front foot. This will give your chip a steeper angle and allow the club to descend on the ball and pop it onto the green.

Bob notes that even fairway woods can be used to chip the ball around the green. The wood's design allows the club to slide through the grass easily, and the loft gets the ball up just enough to start it rolling, producing a rolling and very controllable chip. Bob says that this technique is particularly useful if the ball is in the rough just off the green and points out that Tiger Woods has been using this technique for some time with his usual success. The bottom line, according to Bob, is that a chip shot with a putting-type stroke is low risk and with practice can be high reward.

A fairway wood can be an effective club to use when you are in the rough, just a step or two off the green. Just try to "brush the grass." The heavy, even sole of the fairway wood will help it slide through the rough.

Pitching

Bob teaches that the pitch shot is really a miniswing used with either a pitching wedge or a sand wedge. If you are an average golfer, he says, you may have more success with a pitching wedge. According to him, the size of the swing is determined by the distance of the shot. For example, a shot of 40 yards may require a half backswing, while a 60-yard shot may need a three-quarter-length backswing. Bob finds that a key to this shot is to accelerate through the ball. Many of his students, he says, swing the club back too long in the backswing and then try to slow down and shorten the follow-through to judge the distance. This usually results in a variety of poor shots.

Bob teaches that the proper setup will help you produce and repeat a correct pitch shot. The ball should be positioned in the center to slightly back of center in your stance, depending on how high the ball is sitting in the grass. A poor lie will require that you position the ball a little farther back in the stance. On a full swing, he says, your body should be parallel to the target, while on a pitch shot, your body should be aligned about twenty degrees left of parallel to the target. Bob feels that the open stance allows the body to move easily toward the target. At address, your sternum should be over the ball and your weight should favor the front foot. Bob finds that this is critical to achieving a downward strike of the ball, which allows the club's loft to get the ball up into the air. He feels that many golfers put too much weight on the back foot; as a result, the clubhead comes into the ball too shallow and scoops under it.

Bob likes to use the handle of the golf club as the barometer for the size swing that you need. For example, he says, a short 20-yard pitch shot requires a short swing, so he teaches that you should grip down

> Varying the amount you shorten the handle is an easy way to vary the size of your swing.

on the handle, almost to the shaft. This reminds you to shorten the backswing and also, he notes, a shorter club produces shorter and lower shots. For a 40-yard shot, he teaches that you should hold the club halfway up the handle. A 60-yard shot needs a bigger swing, and you should grip farther up the handle. Varying the amount you shorten the handle is an easy way to vary the size of your swing.

Lob Shots

Bob says that the lob is one of golf's most difficult shots. Anytime you have to make a big swing to hit the ball a short distance, he says, the risk is great. The lob shot means loft, and Bob recommends that you do everything in your power to attain height. If the lie is conducive for loft—meaning that the ball is sitting well enough in the grass to slide the club under the ball—Bob says that you should use a sand wedge and position the ball slightly forward in the stance. Grip the club all the way up the handle, and then try to make a long, slow backswing. A slow backswing will allow you time to accelerate the downswing, Bob says, and this acceleration provides the height and softness to the shot. If this is a shot you encounter a lot at your course, he suggests that you may want to invest in a 60-degree sand wedge. He says that it will take some practice to gain confidence with this club, but that it's lot easier than opening a sand wedge to find some extra loft. A 60-degree sand wedge requires even more acceleration than the standard sand wedge, so the shot is a little riskier. And, he cautions, if you don't have a good lie, it's best not to attempt the lob shot at all.

> The lob shot means loft, and Bob recommends that you do everything in your power to attain height.

Bunker Shots

Bob thinks that to be a good bunker player, you have to be able to understand the different types of sand you might encounter and then adjust your play accordingly. He recommends that you feel the hardness or softness of the sand with your feet when you walk into the bunker. If the sand is soft, he says, you have to utilize the bounce of the sand wedge. Bob teaches that you have to open or lay back the clubface so that the flange or back of the sole of the wedge will enter the sand first. This keeps the wedge from digging too deeply into the sand. Bob notes that an open clubface in hard sand often results in a line drive over the green, while a square face in soft sand usually ends with a fat shot and the ball staying in the bunker because the leading edge of the club dug down under the ball. If the sand is firm or hard, Bob suggests a different approach: the stance should be square (a line across the toes should be parallel to the line of flight), and the clubface should be square to the target. The clubhead should still enter the sand about an inch behind the ball, but because the sand is firm, Bob thinks that you should exert a little more downward pressure with the clubhead to prevent it bouncing off the sand and mishitting the ball.

For the standard bunker shot, Bob says that you should open the face a little, then take your grip. Next, open your stance a little to get positioned toward the target. For most bunker shots, the ball should be positioned just forward of center. Address the ball with more weight on your forward foot—he says about 60 percent on the forward foot and 40 percent on the rear foot. Bob thinks that this promotes a more upright swing and helps the clubhead enter the sand an inch or two behind the ball. He recommends that you focus on the spot behind the ball, the place where you want the club to enter the sand. In your mind's eye, picture the target. Then, he says, swing the club along your body line and follow through. Bob notes that most golfers tend to stop the club in the sand or to keep the weight on the back foot and wind up scooping under the ball, so be sure to follow your shot through.

A good trick that Bob teaches for bunker shots is to visualize the ball sitting on a tee. Position yourself correctly, and then swing as though you were trying to cut the tee in half. He says that this will help you displace the right amount of sand. Another good tip Bob offers is to always position the ball closer to your highest foot. This works great on uneven lies in sand and turf. If your home course has very soft sand, Bob suggests that an investment in a wedge with more bounce will prove to be very valuable. These wedges have an oversized flange and are specifically made for this purpose.

The Mental Aspect

Bob feels that one of the keys to playing your best possible golf is to stay in the present. It's that feeling of being in the "zone," which he believes is a heightened sense of awareness of the situation. Bob thinks that you have to forget about what happened on the last hole and the last stroke and instead totally focus on the task at hand—the next stroke. According to him, the average golfer often gets ahead of him- or herself and starts to think results (the birdie or par), rather than procedure (executing the next shot). It's not unusual to hit a great drive and think to yourself that you should make a birdie only to misplay the next shot and make a bogey or more. The drive, no matter how well struck, is only a drive, he says, and your focus should be on playing the next shot with total concentration. He notes that expectations get in the way as well, such as expecting to shoot a certain score, whether it be 72, 82, 92, or 122. To play your best, he says, you must not have

> A good trick that Bob teaches for bunker shots is to visualize the ball sitting on a tee. Position yourself correctly, and then swing as though you were trying to cut the tee in half.

> To play your best, he says, you must not have expectations or worry about results. Instead, focus on the correct thought process for each shot, one shot at a time.

expectations or worry about results. Instead, focus on the correct thought process for each shot, one shot at a time.

Handling Pressure

When he discusses handling pressure, Bob relates the story of being with his friend, John Elliott, when John qualified for the PGA Tour in 2004. That qualifier is six grueling rounds that pretty much define if you will have a successful year—or even career. Bob saw that John's secret for making that qualifier was a solid routine. He would determine his yardage, then double-check it. He self-talked his way into selecting the correct club. For example, Bob says, John would say, "I have 158 yards to the hole, 145 to the front, wind a little left to right; I want to carry the ball 150 yards. I like a firm 9 iron." (Bob also says to remember that John is one of the longest hitters on the PGA Tour, that's why his 9 iron goes 150 yards!) Bob noticed that John did this self-talk out loud on all of his shots that week and that it helped him focus on the process, not the result. Bob relates that John never once thought about the result, but rather just a good swing at the moment.

In pressure situations, Bob encourages you to make sure you do the obvious—breathe. This may sound ridiculous, he says, but in many pressure situations players become so tight that they forget to breathe. Panic can set in, hands and knees shake, palms sweat, and the mouth goes dry. According to Bob, the best remedy for this is to slow down and concentrate on your breathing. You should take three or four deep breaths. Try to relax, he says, and then plan your next shot.

25

Susanne Newell

Instructor, The Original Golf School at Mount Snow

The Short Game

Susanne thinks that the short game is an area in which everyone can excel. Strength is not necessary, she says; rather, some sound fundamentals, creativity, and practice will improve your short game. First, you must have a plan. Susanne teaches that you have to visualize the shot you are trying to play. Does the situation require a high soft shot or a low rolling shot? Only after you have painted a good visual picture, she says, can you produce the best possible shot. You can't be successful on the course unless you have practiced with a variety of clubs and feel comfortable with the varying distances and results you achieve with each.

According to Susanne, a good way to gauge all shots around the green is to start with a mental picture of throwing the golf ball under-

Susanne Newell is an instructor with The Original Golf School at Mount Snow Golf Club in West Dover, Vermont, and at the Plantation Golf Resort in Crystal River, Florida. She was voted one of the best teachers in the state of Vermont by *Golf Digest*.

Susanne enjoys both courses for their different beauty. The course at Mount Snow is located in the Green Mountain National Forest, and the views are spectacular. The Plantation Golf Resort is a classic Florida golf course with tropical flowers and a wonderful assortment of wildlife.

hand to a spot on the green and then picture it rolling toward the hole. Then, she says, pick a club that you think will produce that type of flight and roll and execute the shot.

Susanne's final general tip about the short game is that you should keep your arms moving on each stroke around the green. When your arms stop too soon, whether it is a putt, chip, or pitch, the results will not be good.

Putting

Susanne teaches that putting requires a good preshot routine, just like every other stroke. She also says that there are two steps to improved putting: alignment and speed. To make sure your alignment is correct, she says, stand behind the ball and look at the entire line or path to the hole. Then pick an intermediate spot along that line. Address the ball and line up the putter face with that intermediate spot. Your eyes should be over the ball and a line across your shoulders and feet should be parallel to the line of the putt. At this point, Susanne says, the focus now is on the speed of the putt. As you stand over the ball, she recommends that you let your eyes travel up and down that line at the speed you expect the ball to roll. By doing this several times, you give your brain the necessary "input." That way, according to Susanne, your brain knows what to tell your hands to do. When you make the putt, she says that you should hit the ball with enough speed to go past the hole a foot or two if it does not go in.

The best putters pick an intermediate spot on the green and putt over that spot, toward the hole.

Chipping

Susanne says that the chip shot is a good, reliable way to get the ball close to the hole from slightly off the green, maybe two to four steps. She proposes the following fundamentals for chipping:

1. Use a narrower stance than your normal iron shot.
2. Make sure the ball is in the back of the stance to ensure that the club will hit the ball before it strikes the turf.
3. Position your hands slightly ahead of the ball at address.
4. Put your weight on the front foot.
5. Keep your head steady throughout the stroke.
6. Make sure there is no weight movement below the waist.
7. Set the club a little on the toe, not soled as in the regular fairway shot, to allow the club to slide through uneven clumps of grass. When the club catches, it is always the heel that catches first, so tip the chipping iron up on its toe and it won't get snagged by the grass.
8. Make sure your eyes are over the ball, as in putting.
9. Keep your grip pressure soft.

> You can't be successful on the course unless you have practiced with a variety of clubs and feel comfortable with the varying distances and results you achieve with each.

Pitching

Susanne notes that the pitch is a little longer than the chip. She suggests that you pick a landing spot that allows for sufficient roll.

According to her, many golfers choose a spot that is too far into the green; however, even pitch shots will roll quite a bit. She encourages you to visualize the shot by getting back to the idea of an underhand toss of a ball landing on the green and then rolling toward the hole. Where you visualize the ball landing, she says, will be the ball's actual landing spot.

The fundamentals of the pitch shot that Susanne teaches are the following:

1. You should adopt an open stance. Your feet should be open to the target and your shoulders should be square.
2. There should be some wrist hinge on this shot (this will occur automatically, she says, if you have the correct grip and you are not holding the club too tightly). There is a hinge on the backswing, but not on the follow-through.
3. The length of the backswing controls the distance. The longer the backswing, the farther the ball will go.
4. All of your swings should have the same tempo.
5. Your hands should be over the ball at address.
6. The ball should be positioned in the center of your stance.
7. The torso and club move together on the backswing, and the chest faces the target on the follow-through, as in a full swing.
8. There is a hinge of the wrists on the backswing, but not on the follow-through.

Bunker Shots

Susanne teaches that, when you are playing a bunker shot, you need to customize your technique to the type of lie you have. If you have a good lie, she says, the ball position is a little more forward so you can make contact with the sand behind the ball.

Good acceleration on the follow-through is what will give the ball some height. A tip that she offers to help you avoid hitting the ball before the sand is to bend both elbows slightly at the address position. Your arms will then extend from the force of the swing and you'll be assured of hitting the sand before you strike the ball. She also notes that a follow-through will help your bunker game become more consistent.

When the ball is in a lie in a sand bunker that is not good—in a footprint, for example, or just down in the sand—Susanne teaches that you have to change your approach. In this situation, she notes that you have to dig the clubhead down into the sand so that the leading edge of the club gets below the ball. To create this digging action, she says, square your stance, position the ball back in the stance (off the back foot), and then just bury the clubhead down below the ball. The swing will be steep, the clubhead will get down below the ball, and the downward pressure of the club and loft of the club will pop the ball up. Susanne notes that this is one of the few times in golf that you don't and actually can't follow through—the club is digging so steeply into the sand that the follow-through is not possible.

The Mental Aspect

Susanne thinks that much of golf is played between the player's two ears, so she offers a trick for getting into a better mental approach. How often, she asks, do you hear players say that they were great on the front nine and terrible on the back nine (or just the opposite, bad on the front and good on the back)? She

Whenever the ball is depressed (in other words, in a footprint or embedded) in the greenside bunker, the technique is different than in a level lie. Address the ball in the back of the stance and swing abruptly down behind the ball. The loft of the club and the downward pressure of the club will force the ball into the air.

acknowledges that there is some barrier or relief players feel when changing nine holes. While she doesn't know if anyone can really explain it, it's there. She speculates that it may be the idea of a "fresh start" on the tenth tee if the round is not going well or the feeling of "I can't believe I'm playing this well." Susanne recommends dividing the eighteen holes into three six-hole segments instead of two nines. If you play the first six holes poorly, she says, focus on the next six holes—you may regain your steam and be ready for a career finish on the last six holes.

26

Pete Mathews

Head Professional, Western View Golf Club

Putting

Pete says that his specialty in teaching putting is the use of the long putter. Pete relates that when he had his first case of nerves in a tournament in 1984, he tried all of the common methods to get back on track. The method that he found and the one he now passes on to other players is the use of the long putter. This technique requires the specially made putters that are long enough to anchor the handle on your chest. Pete recommends that you help that anchor with your left hand holding the end of the putter, and extend your right arm so that it controls the swinging action of the putter, much like a pendulum in a grandfather clock. Pete teaches this style as the best way to putt because there are so few moving parts.

Pete Mathews is the head professional at Western View Golf Club in Augusta, Maine. Pete has won the Vermont Senior PGA Championship as well as the Maine Senior PGA Championship three times.

Western View is a challenging course with an appropriate name, as you can see most of the beautiful Maine mountain range west of the course.

Just like that grandfather clock, you swing the putter back and forth at an even pace.

Pete thinks that developing a feel for distance with the long putter takes some practice but that this is not a difficult task. The even, swinging action of the pendulum creates a very reliable roll on the ball that is easy to control. The advantage to this system is that there is not too much that can go wrong. Pete says that you just line it up and swing the pendulum. This simplicity creates confidence in starting the putt on line and controlling the distance, and as he says, confidence is the key to good putting. As soon as negative thoughts creep in, he notes, you have little chance of being successful.

Pete teaches that making the all important short putts once again is a product of confidence. Have no doubt in the line or the speed. If you feel uncertain, he says, step back, reread the putt, and begin your preshot routine all over again. A great drill that he recommends for short putts is to "push" the ball into the hole from 3 feet. Take no backswing at all and push the ball into the hole. (This is a drill, he cautions, and unfortunately cannot be done in normal play.) Pete thinks that this exercise will help you get the feeling of the putter head going toward the hole and also help you realize how small a backstroke is required to hit a 3-foot putt.

> If you feel uncertain, he says, step back, reread the putt, and begin your preshot routine all over again.

Pitching and Chipping

Pete says that pitching and chipping are stroke savers and that there is no real substitute for practice. When he is teaching these shots, he wants you to think more about focus than mechanics. He notes that it's so easy to lose focus when you hit chip after chip from the same spot in a practice session, so he advises that you vary the situations and shot selections to keep yourself focused.

Pete has a few key pointers for these shots: always have a plan, know where you want to land the ball, and know how much roll you anticipate. For most players, the best plan is to have the ball roll as much as possible, so he recommends playing most chip strokes with about a 7 iron. As the length of the shot increases, he says, you'll require a little more swing. The bigger swing will feel like you're putting a little more body into the shot. He notes that the club selection for the pitch shot should be the pitching wedge for most golfers, although advanced golfers can use the pitching wedge, gap wedge, sand wedge, or lob wedge, depending on the situation.

The Mental Aspect

As Pete says, to improve as a player you have to be decisive and have confidence in yourself. Don't overanalyze what you do, he cautions, as too much thinking is not good. Instead, he advises that you rely on your tempo. Take a look at the situation, have confidence in your instincts, loosen up, and make a swing.

> To improve as a player you have to be decisive and have confidence in yourself.

27

Bob Kay

Teaching Professional, Citrus Hills Golf Course

Putting

There are two basic rules that Bob relays when he is teaching putting. First, your head should not move during the stroke because any head motion will influence the swinging action of the putter. He says that a good trick is to keep your head still during the stroke and listen for the pleasing sound of the ball hitting the bottom of the cup. Second, the putter should be swung at the hole and the ball should just get in the way. In fact, Bob recommends that you totally forget that the ball is there. Just stroke the putter to the hole, he says, and eliminate the ball in the equation. The weight and swinging action of the putter move the ball to the hole.

Bob Kay is the teaching professional at Citrus Hills Golf Course in Hernando, Florida. Bob was an outstanding college player, making the College All American Team, Division 2. As a professional, Bob has won the Vermont PGA twice as well as the New Hampshire PGA.

Citrus Hills is a fifty-four-hole complex. The courses are The Oaks, The Meadows, and Sky Line at Terra Vista. The fairways are lined with large Southern live oaks and Spanish moss hangs from their branches, giving the courses a real Southern feel. The courses also enjoy good elevation changes and rolling hills, which is very unusual anywhere in Florida.

Chipping

According to Bob, the chip shot is very similar to a putt but is hit slightly on the downstroke. To produce that slightly different stroke, he says, you need to change the address position. Your hands should be forward of the ball and there should be more weight on your front foot. He also recommends that your hands stay ahead of the clubhead throughout the swing. To help you achieve the feeling of the wrist not hinging during the chip, Bob teaches that the back of your left hand should swing toward the target. If the wrists incorrectly hinge, he says, the back of the left hand will face the sky.

Bob advises that it's a good idea to learn to use a variety of clubs to chip with. It gives you a wider variety of options and, as Bob says, "that's why they make all those clubs."

Pitching

Bob teaches the same fundamentals with the pitch shot that he does with the full swing. Your body and arms move together. He says that there is not too much motion with the legs because not much of a weight shift is required on a short pitch—there should be just enough weight shift to support the swing. Bob teaches that you should keep your head behind the ball so that there is no lateral motion in the swing.

Bunker Shots

When you have to make a sand shot, Bob recommends that you take a grounded stance in the bunker. Dig your feet into the stance to get a more stable base and also to get a feel for the amount of sand in the bunker. So often, he says, you'll see nice white, fluffy sand only to find out that underneath that thin layer of white sand is very hard ground. While the rules of golf do not permit you to test the sand, he notes that you are entitled to take a fair stance and in so doing you can feel with your feet what is under that white, fluffy sand.

Bob teaches that you need to use the bounce or sole of the club properly to be a good bunker player. The sole will help the club glide through the sand. To use the bounce, he says, you should open the stance and aim the face of the club at the target. The wedge will be laid back and the bounce of the wedge will be close to the sand.

Bob advises that you maintain an even pace during the swing—there should be no accelerating or decelerating. He says that you should always use a fairly long backswing in a bunker shot. According to him, the length of the follow-through will determine the length of the shot.

> While the rules of golf do not permit you to test the sand, he notes that you are entitled to take a fair stance and in so doing you can feel with your feet what is under that white, fluffy sand.

The Mental Aspect

Bob teaches that it is very important to stay positive. The one thing he knows for sure, he says, is that "negative thinking really works, it definitely will produce negative results." Instead, he recommends that you learn how to stay positive. Every player is different, he cautions, and there is no automatic way to teach everyone to think positive thoughts. But you should be able to picture good golf shots, execute a good swing, and not let the fear of failure be part of your game.

28

John Buczek

Head Professional, Winged Foot Golf Club

Chipping

John teaches that chipping is really putting, for the most part, with various clubs with different lofts. John has a simple and easy formula to remember the mechanics of chipping: two lefts and a right. Your hands are positioned over your inside left leg at address, weight should be slightly on your left foot, and the ball should be positioned off your right foot. He notes that the width of the stance should only be 5 to 10 inches.

For this shot, John says, the correct motion is to swing with your arms and shoulders, brushing the grass with the sole of the club. The hands and wrists just hold on to the club. If you use too much hand action, he cautions, you will change the path and loft of the club

John Buczek is the head professional at Winged Foot Golf Club in Mamaroneck, New York. John started his professional career working for the legendary Claude Harmon at Winged Foot. John then moved on to be the head professional at Crestmont Country Club and then at Plainfield Country Club, both in New Jersey. While there, John won the New Jersey Open and the New Jersey PGA Championship. He was the New Jersey PGA Player of the Year in 1975. After moving to Grandfather Golf and Country Club in North Carolina, John received the Professional of the Year Award and the Teacher of the Year Award from the North Carolina PGA section.

and thus you will not hit the ball before the turf, as you should.

John suggests that you experiment with a variety of clubs to get a feel for how much loft and roll each club will produce. For example, he says, a 7 iron will probably propel the ball 25 percent in the air and 75 percent on the ground. The sand wedge, on the other hand, will be the opposite, sending the ball 75 percent in the air and 25 percent on the ground.

Pitching

John notes that once you move back from the green, 8 yards or more, you have to use a more lofted club to carry the area before the green and land the ball safely on the green. The ball will land softly with little roll. To make this shot, he says, you should choose a club with plenty of loft. Wedges are made with different lofts ranging from 48 degrees to 60 degrees. The idea of all wedges is to take a similar swing with the different lofts to produce higher or lower trajectories, so John recommends that you not try to change your swing to hit the ball higher or lower, but instead change clubs.

When playing pitch shots, John teaches that you should address the ball in the center of the stance, with your hands slightly forward. (He notes that you can experiment gripping the handle a bit shorter for shorter distances.) When you swing, he says, make an effort to clip the grass at the bottom of the swing, striking the ball and then the turf. Finally, he advises, allow the body to turn back and through, although the amount of body turn will vary with the distance you are trying to achieve.

Remember, John cautions, that the wedges have the loft built in to the clubface, so you need to trust the club to put the ball in the air. He emphasizes that there is no need to try to help the ball get airborne. Hitting down makes the ball go up!

> There is no need to try to help the ball get airborne. Hitting down makes the ball go up!

Bunker Shots

John's golden rule of sand play is that you should hit the sand before the ball. If you hit too much sand first, he says, you won't have too far to walk to the next shot!

Here is how John teaches the sand shot: The sand wedge will have some bounce on the sole to allow the club to slide through the sand without digging too deeply. Play this stroke with the clubface open, even pointing to the right. The ball should be forward of center in the stance. He recommends that you have the clubhead enter the sand 2 to 3 inches behind the ball and follow through; throw the sand and the ball onto the green. John also notes that the bunker should be played with a long, lazy swing.

29

Sal Ruggiero

Teaching Professional, Ibis Golf and Country Club

Putting

Sal thinks that the art of putting is 30 percent proper mechanics and 70 percent positive thinking, confidence, tempo, and the ability to read the break and speed of the greens. Sal also finds that grip pressure is important—it should be very light so that you can feel the weight of the head of the putter. Light grip pressure will help you keep the stroke smooth, he says, and will give you the best chance to get a feel for speed. While there are certainly many ways to grip the putter, Sal usually teaches the reverse overlap grip. In this grip, the index finger of your top hand overlaps the pinky, ring, and middle fingers of the bottom hand.

When you are putting, Sal suggests that the width of your stance be less than the width of your shoulders. He teaches that you should

Sal Ruggiero is the teaching professional at Ibis Golf and Country Club in West Palm Beach, Florida. Sal has been voted the New England PGA Teacher of the Year. As a player, Sal has a very impressive record. He holds the course record of 62 at the Plantation Golf Resort in Crystal River, Florida. He also won the New England Senior PGA Championship and the PGA National Stroke Play Championship (60–65 age division).

Ibis Golf and Country Club is a beautiful, Jack Nicklaus–designed, fifty-four-hole complex in West Palm Beach, Florida.

The reverse overlap grip, pictured here, is the most popular and traditional way to hold the handle of the putter. Both thumbs are on top of the shaft, the palms are opposing, and the forefinger of the top hand extends down along the fingers of the bottom hand.

putt from a slightly open stance. Most of your weight should be on your front foot, as this will keep the lower part of your body still. To achieve the correct motion, he teaches that the putter should be swung with the triangle formed by your arms and a line across your shoulders. The feeling, he says, is that you're moving the sternum in tempo with the putter head. This system keeps the stroke smooth and the clubhead on line.

Chipping

Sal teaches the same approach for chipping that he uses for putting. The only difference is that he recommends that you use several different clubs—actually, any club in the range from a 5 iron to a sand wedge. He advises that you shorten up on the handle to make whatever club you use be about the same length as your putter. Then hold the club more perpendicular to the ground, so the club sits on its toe. Brush down through the grass and the ball, he says, with a short follow-through. Sal advises that you think of this approach as having three or four putters in the bag, each with a different loft. A good general rule, he says, is to choose a club when chipping that will land the ball on and not before the green.

Pitching

For most pitch shots, Sal use the simple "toe-up, toe-up" swing. In this approach, when swinging, your hands should go from about waist high to waist high. If the club has been swung correctly, he says, the toe of the club will point toward the sky on the backswing and then toward the sky on the follow-through. And at the end of the swing, your weight should finish on your forward foot so that the heel of your back foot is off the ground and observers can see the golf spikes on your shoes. Your balance point will be on the toe of the back foot, hence the name, the "toe-up, toe-up" swing.

Sal points out that this system is also a great drill for the long game. The finish position will give you all of the input you need if you are having trouble with the full swing. If you finish the swing incorrectly, for instance, with your body weight on your back foot instead of your front foot, this drill is a good, simple way to correct the flaw. The correction would be to work on the weight shift, making sure that you transfer your weight to your back foot on the backswing and to your front foot on the forward swing. If you are having trouble with the game, Sal says, in general, it is easier to cure it with this drill than by whaling away with a driver at the range.

> If the club has been swung correctly, he says, the toe of the club will point toward the sky on the backswing and then toward the sky on the follow-through.

Lob Shots

Sal notes that a soft, flop, or lob shot is sometimes required when you have very little green to work with and you have to hit the ball almost straight up. The sand wedge is the more traditional club used for this task. A few points that Sal emphasizes when making this shot are to keep your legs still, as no extra leg action is needed; to open the clubface of the sand wedge; and with dead hands (no wrist break), to slide the club through the ball on the downswing.

To produce a high, soft shot around the green, you have to rely on the loft of the club to get the ball airborne. A long, slow swing with light grip pressure will achieve the best results.

Notice how the arms are fully extended, the head is still "quiet," and the swinging action of the club pops the ball into the air.

With this shot, he says, you will get the feeling that the ball is rolling off the back of the clubface.

The Mental Aspect

Sal feels that it's very important to just hit one shot at a time, and then to focus on the next shot. You should block out everything else, he says, and visualize the type of shape and type of shot you want to execute. Then try to make a smooth, balanced swing. Stay positive, he advises, and don't get ahead of yourself.

Greg Loniewski

General Manager and Director of Golf,
Glen Riddle Golf Club

The Putting Grip

Greg feels that putting is highly preferential in nature, noting that no two great putters ever seem to go about the task exactly the same way. Even with this in mind, however, he believes that most players who are great putters have a handful of things in common.

For starters, he says, when you think about the putting grip, the word *grip* sends the wrong message. You should not "grip" the handle of the putter, but rather place it in your palms, as though you were caressing it.

Greg teaches that it's not the firmness with which you hold the club that produces a solid stroke. Let your arms and hands relax and hang somewhat naturally from your shoulders, he says, and simply rotate your shoulders, produc-

Greg Loniewski is the General Manager and Director of Golf at Glen Riddle Golf Club in Ocean City, Maryland. Greg has operated golf schools in Ocean City, Maryland, Sugarbush, Vermont, and Manchester, Vermont. He has helped thousands of students, including some PGA Tour players.

Glen Riddle is an upscale, thirty-six-hole complex on the Sam Riddle farm, which was famous for being the home of two of the most famous racehorses, Man o' War and War Admiral. The two courses are named for these great horses.

The reverse overlap putting grip.

ing a one-piece rocking motion. He notes that there is no wrist action in this putting stroke; the putter is swung by the action of the arms and shoulders.

Greg thinks that it is a fatal misconception to minimize excessive wrist and hand action by merely firming the grip and arms. Great putters generally adopt a hand position that by itself restricts unwanted motion. The reverse overlap, claw, palms skyward, and cross-handed grips are some of the many putting grip variations used to keep the hands quiet. Keep in mind, he says, that it's usually a good putter who uses a somewhat funny-looking putting grip.

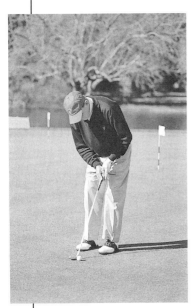
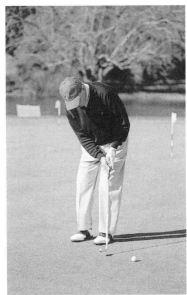

The putting stroke should be the simple swinging of the putter with your arms and shoulders. It is very important to have soft grip pressure. To improve your putting, you must have a "feel" for distance and direction, which can only happen if you hold the handle lightly, as you would a pool cue.

SHORT GAME SECRETS OF THE PROS

Putting Stance and Alignment

As in most golf shots, Greg says, the way that you stand up to the ball and address it is extremely important. By stance, he is not only talking about your feet; rather, your feet, knees, hips, shoulders, hands, and even your eyes need to be in good stance and alignment. Your feet should be placed either square (parallel to the line of the putt) or open (aligned to the left). Greg feels that your stance should never be closed (aligned to the right of the target line) when you putt, as a square or open stance both allow the free rotation of the shoulders and allow the putter head to be swung toward the target. With a closed stance, he warns, your arms and shoulders can no longer rotate together, extension of your arms is lost, and the putter will be pulled up and in, away from the target.

> Your feet, knees, hips, shoulders, hands, and even your eyes need to be in good stance and alignment.

Greg thinks that the width of the stance is not very important; he does point out, however, that a very narrow or very wide stance will help minimize lower body rotation. He also says that putting all of your weight on your left foot or right foot or even using a knock-kneed address position will also go a long way in helping you stay quiet below the waist, a trait that is universal in great putters. Bend at the waist, he advises, or get close enough to the ball so that your eyes are looking directly over the ball. Your eyes need not be directly over the ball—they could be behind the ball somewhat—but they must be on the target line.

The Putting Stroke

Greg teaches that the putting stroke might be better described as a short swing. With a sound relaxed "grip" and a one-piece rotation of the shoulders, hands, and arms, the putter should be "swung" back from and through to the target. The ball merely gets in the way of the swinging putter.

Putting Rhythm

Greg thinks that the putting stroke, like full shots, should have a certain rhythm. According to him, a smooth-flowing, never-changing tempo ensures a putting stroke that will never break down. A short putt, with a short stroke and a nice rhythm, will propel the ball a short distance on a straight line. A longer putt, with a longer stroke and the same nice rhythm, will propel the ball a longer distance on a straight line. Greg says to keep the same rhythm, just vary the length of the stroke to fit the distance.

Target Orientation

Greg relates a good story about "target orientation." Years ago, he came upon a four-year-old boy on the practice green at Manchester Country Club. The dad had left the boy under the watchful eye of a club member so he could play a quick nine holes. When the father returned, he saw that his son had attracted a crowd of golfers watching the boy sink putts from all over the green. They were all amazed and asked the four-year-old for his secret. The boy looked puzzled, obviously not understanding the question. He said, "Dad, all I'm really trying to do is get the ball in the hole."

With all of the worry about the stroke, grip, and everything that goes with it, Greg says, "maybe, just maybe, we should just try to put the ball in the hole." His point is that if you concentrate on the target, many of the mechanics will fall into place.

Bob Hogarth

Head Professional, The Royal Montreal Golf Club

31

Putting

Bob had the pleasure of playing with and learning his golf from the great short-game specialist Paul Runyan. Bob has adopted the Runyan Method, which teaches that short strokes around the green should be played with the one-lever system. This means that there should be no wrist hinge for putts, chips, or very short pitches. Bob suggests that, to use this method, you will need to alter the way you hold the club. Your hands should be turned outward so that the palms of your hands are facing the sky. He notes that this change "locks" the hands so that there will be no wrist hinge. When you putt, he says, you just move your shoulders in a rocking motion so that the swing has no hand action. According to Bob, this method produces a smooth stroke, making it easy to

Bob Hogarth is the head professional at The Royal Montreal Golf Club in Montreal, Canada, and is one of the best teachers and players in the Montreal area. Bob has won several local Canadian PGA championships. He has developed his teaching skills based on his work with two of the most respected teachers in golf, Paul Runyan and Jim Hardy.

The Royal Montreal Golf Club is the oldest club in North America. It was started in 1873, well before any of the famous older courses in the United States. It has hosted the Canadian Open eight times and will be the site of the prestigious Presidents Cup in 2007.

control distances, and also makes putting the "short ones" easier as the stroke has no moving parts.

Chipping and Pitching

Bob teaches that to chip or to hit very short pitches with the Runyon Method, you have to make one adjustment at the address position. As this style of chipping is so close to putting, he says, you have to move closer to the ball than you would with the standard grip. When you set the iron on the grass, it will sit a little on its toe. Bob notes that to play a short pitch shot, you should use a standard putting grip. This method will make all shots like a putt. He says that it's a reliable shot, particularly under pressure.

As the shots get longer, however, maybe more than 10 yards, Bob says that you will have to abandon the Runyan grip and return to the standard grip you use on full shots. The regular grip will keep the clubface square, which will give you the necessary loft for longer pitch shots.

A Specialty Shot

A unique shot that Bob learned from Paul Runyan was one that he called his "underreaching shot." Bob says that he never did receive the full explanation of how Paul Runyan named this specialty shot, but he has found it to be very useful. One of the most difficult short shots, he notes, is one from very hard

> When you putt, he says, you just move your shoulders in a rocking motion so that the swing has no hand action.

The short pitch can actually be played as you would a very long putt. Select a wedge and use your putting grip and stance, which will be fairly close to the ball. The club will be sitting more on its toe than normal. Now use a long, smooth putting stroke. The ball will get plenty of loft and come out softly.

ground near the green. Bob relates that this is how Paul would play it: he would address the ball normally, then raise his spine ever so slightly, perhaps only one quarter of an inch. This slight adjustment would prevent him from hitting behind the ball. According to Bob, this is a great way to ensure clean contact from a hard ground lie.

Bunker Shots

To play a bunker shot from a good lie, Bob suggests that you play the ball forward in the stance and aim a little left (for right-handed players) as there will be some cut or slice spin on the ball. The most important part of this shot, he says, is to focus on the sand splashing out of the bunker. Bob feels that too many golfers focus on trying to scoop the ball out of the bunker when all they really have to do is splash the sand and the ball will come out.

To play a bunker shot from a poor lie, Bob suggests that you "toe" the club in—a lot—so that the toe, not the clubface, is aimed at the ball. When the toe enters the sand, he says, it will easily cut through the sand and the clubhead will get down below the ball, forcing the ball up and out. Bob also notes that soft hands will help to create a soft shot and prevent a low running ball flight.

Flop Shots

A good tip that Bob offers for producing a high soft shot around the green is to have soft grip pressure. Any type of tightness in the grip will produce a low and driving ball flight. So for the desired soft, high shot around the green, he says, use soft grip pressure and make a long, slow smooth swing.

Handling Pressure

Take the practice swing with the same intent and focus you will have for the next stroke.

Bob relates a good tip in handling pressure. He feels that the practice swing is your only friend while you are actually in a competitive golf situation. (And, he notes, competitive golf can be very lonely.) He recommends that you use the practice swing as a rehearsal for the next stroke. Get a feel for how hard you will swing. Brush the grass a few times. Take the practice swing with the same intent and focus you will have for the next stroke. Then when it's your turn to play, he says, try to reproduce that feel—it works and it's a great way to break the tension.

Paul Marquis

Professional, Rheinfelden Golf Platz

32

Paul Marquis is the golf professional at Rheinfelden Golf Platz in Basil, Switzerland. He is one of the true pioneers in Swiss golf instruction, having been a top instructor in the first golf school in Switzerland, the Golf School at Schlossgut Eppishausen Golf & Country Club in Erlen, Switzerland.

Rheinfelden Golf Platz is one of the finest golf training centers in Switzerland. It has state-of-the-art teaching aids and a nine-hole course to test new skills. Rheinfelden has all the latest teaching aids and they are in the process of developing a course so golfers can test their new skills.

Chipping and Pitching

Paul says that he teaches more of a "chip and run" style as it seems to suit the courses in Switzerland better than the higher greenside shots that are needed on more American-style courses. He suggests the simple one-lever putting style approach to all of the "pitch and run" strokes around the green, for shots within about 15 yards. For shots longer than 15 yards, Paul suggests that you use the standard grip to produce sufficient clubhead speed to get height on the shot.

Paul stresses good balance in all short shots around the green, feeling that most shots are missed when balance is lost. Paul has a unique method to help students gain clubface awareness. He assigns numbers to different areas of the clubface: #1 is the toe of the club; #2 is the middle of the club, the "sweet spot"; #3 is the inside of the clubface; and #4 is the bottom of the clubface. Of course, Paul recognizes that everyone would like to hit the ball on #2, the sweet spot, but that's not likely. Paul suggests that you address the ball on #1, the toe. You will most likely either strike the ball near the toe, which will produce a good to fair result, or in the sweet spot, which will produce the best result. He thinks that this system decreases the chance that you will strike the ball on the inside of the clubface (the dreaded shank) or the bottom of the clubface (the almost-as-dreaded ground ball).

Paul Marquis teaches that the easiest way to achieve good results with uneven lies in the bunker is to make sure the line across your shoulders matches the slope of the hill or bunker. In the uphill shot, the ball will fly higher, and in the downhill shot, it will naturally fly lower. You have to develop a feel for the changes in flight and then play accordingly.

Bunker Shots

Paul says that many bunker shots are mishit because the player does not properly adjust to the slope of the bunker. What should be natural, he claims, is to follow the slope of the hill. Thus, when you address the bunker shot, he recommends that an imaginary line drawn across your shoulders should be at the same angle as the slope of the bunker. Paul says that when you are playing from an uphill lie in the bunker, the club will have extra loft when you assume an address. For example, the 56-degree wedge will become 60- or more degrees just because you are following the slope. Thus, he says, the adjustment you have to make is to swing harder. Just the reverse is true for downhill bunker shots, he notes. The sand wedge will have decreased loft, so you have to swing soft and smooth on this shot.

Doug Dalziel

PGA Senior Tour

Putting

Doug feels that to some degree, good putters are "natural," that they have a feel that is built in. To be a good putter, he says, you have to be comfortable at the address position, confident in your line, and certain that you can make the putt.

Doug thinks that if you try to be too mechanical, you simply will not have enough "feel" to be a consistent putter. He feels that instead, you have to be comfortable and then trust your instincts. According to him, the mechanics of putting are simple: the putter blade should swing straight back from the target and straight through to the target. The distance you roll the ball is determined by the size of the putting stroke. The length of the stroke going back

Doug Dalziel hails from one of golf's true legendary homes, Carnoustie Golf Club, in Carnoustie, Scotland. Among Doug's numerous accomplishments are winning two Connecticut Opens, two Connecticut PGA Championships, and the National Senior Stroke Play championship as well as being a runner-up in the British Senior Open. Doug has spent most of his professional career in the United States as a club professional and as a full-time player on the PGA Senior Tour.

Carnoustie is one of Scotland's most difficult and cherished courses. It was the site of the 1953 British Open that was won by Ben Hogan. It was Ben's only trip to the British Open, and he was making a successful comeback from his near-fatal accident.

A comfortable address position is a key to being a good putter, as you are trying to produce a smooth stroke with some touch. Try to find an address position that feels good to you. Your arms should be hanging comfortably and your grip pressure should be soft. Once you have achieved that good address position, Doug Dalziel suggests that you just trust your instincts.

Once you have a good address position, make a long, smooth, even stroke. Notice that the head is stationary long after the putt has been struck.

should match the length of the stroke going forward, much like the pendulum of a grandfather clock.

A good tip that Doug offers is this: if you have good peripheral vision, watch the head of the putter as it swings back and through. That will get your mind off the ball and help you visualize a good putting stroke.

Chipping and Pitching

Doug teaches a unique method of chipping and pitching the ball. He tries to create a very even motion for these strokes, one with no acceleration or deceleration. To create this shot, he recommends addressing the ball with some weight on the forward foot. When you swing, you will feel some motion with your left (forward) hip; try to time that motion with the swing and speed of your arms. By moving everything together, he says, you create a true pendulum.

There is no reason to use your hands with this shot as the club is being swung by the big muscles—your arms, shoulders, and hips. With both the chip and pitch, Doug teaches that the ball position should be just back of center to ensure solid contact.

Bunker Shots

Doug feels that the bunker shot is very important as many players aim away from the sand, often heading toward more dangerous territory. It is really an easy shot, he claims, as you're just moving a divot of sand out of the bunker; if the ball is anywhere in that divot, it, too, will come out. The ball should be played slightly forward in the stance, according to him, and you should have a little more weight on your back foot (60 percent) than your front foot. Doug suggests that keeping your weight more on the back foot at address will ensure that you hit the necessary inch or two behind the ball, preventing you from hitting the ball first and sending it sailing over the green.

Even in short shots, the club is swung using the bigger muscles of the arms and shoulders. Here the golfer also shows how to move your left hip in sync with your arms and shoulders. This helps keep any quick wrist action out of the swing and makes you rely on the bigger muscles.

Soft grip pressure

is the key to

being successful

when you are in

any competitive

situation.

Handling Pressure

Doug believes that soft grip pressure is the key to being successful when you are in any competitive situation. He says that your grip pressure should be so light that your playing partner could easily pull the club out of your hand. Light pressure will help you feel the club and maintain flexibility.

Don Hachey

Professional, Beaconsfield Golf Club

34

Putting

Don feels that most recreational golfers use their hands too much as they putt. He teaches students to rely on swinging the putter with arms and shoulders; your hands just hold on to the handle. To improve alignment, Don suggests that you make a chalk line on the green and then square the putter blade to that line. The chalk line will tell you if you are lined up correctly. If you are misaligned at the chalk line, Don says, you will appear to be aimed to the right or left of the target. This is a great tool to help you regain good awareness of the line to the hole.

The putting drill that Don has had the most success with is this: place four balls around the hole, 3 feet from the hole at the four points of the compass. Then go "around

Don Hachey is the golf professional at Beaconsfield Golf Club in Point Clair, Montreal, Canada. Don Hachey has been named the Quebec Province Canadian PGA Professional of the Year. Don qualified for the Canadian Open and has won four times on the Quebec PGA Tour.

Beaconsfield is one of the oldest and most prestigious golf clubs in Canada. Founded in 1902, it has been at the same site since 1904.

> Make a chalk line on the green and then square the putter blade to that line. The chalk line will tell you if you are lined up correctly.

the horn," trying to make all four putts. Once you do this successfully, Don says, move the balls back to 4 feet. The idea is to see how far from the hole you can move and make all four putts. This drill increases feel and gains confidence.

Chipping and Pitching

Don uses and teaches a unique system for short shots around the green. It is partly derived from a teacher, Mindy Blake, and a current golf guru, Jim Hardy. Don teaches that the club should be swung low and inside the path on the backswing, not straight back and straight through on the forward swing. He thinks that too many players, in an attempt to swing the club straight back, actually lift the club with their hands and swing the club too much on the outside of the desired line of flight. Taking the clubhead low and inside with no wrist break, he says, will create a slightly "closed" clubface. (If you were wearing a wristwatch, the face of the watch would be facing the ground on the backswing.) On the forward swing, there is no wrist break. He notes that the lower body initiates the downswing, and your body turns toward the target. As there is no wrist hinge and the club is swung with the larger muscles, he says, the ball flight will be high and soft.

Bunker Shots

Don feels that most players have a fear of "laying the face of the sand wedge open," so they wind up not using the bounce of the wedge effectively. Once you are properly set up, he suggests that you swing the club with no release. Don feels that the clubface should be pointed toward the sky on the follow-through. The concept of pulling down the handle will help you to keep the clubface open during the swing. If the clubface closes in the hitting area, he says, the club will not bounce through the sand but will instead dig into the sand and get stuck. This results in no follow-through, and it becomes impossible to hit the divot of sand onto the green—and, unfortunately, the ball and the sand will stay in the bunker. Instead, you should use the bounce of the wedge to slide the clubhead through the sand, creating a full follow-through.

Handling Pressure

Don says that the best way to handle pressure is to breathe. Breathe deep, he says, so that you can feel the lower abdomen expand. It will help you relax your entire body.

Don's second trick is that you make an effort to "slow down." In the heat of battle, he says, it is natural to walk quicker and talk faster. Instead, he recommends that you relax, take your time, and control your mannerisms so that you don't get ahead of yourself. Slowing down your mannerisms will help you maintain good tempo in your swing and putting stroke.

> The best way to handle pressure is to breathe. Breathe deep, he says, so that you can feel the lower abdomen expand. It will help you relax your entire body.

Some Final Thoughts

35

My purpose in this book was to give you more confidence in the short game. Confidence is having the knowledge to perform with the addition of some intelligent practice. I hope that the information from these many fine professional teachers will provide you with the know-how to improve your short game.

Practice is the next step. A good rule is to practice your short game at least as much as your long game. While it may be more fun to hit drivers at the range, spending equal time on the short game will have a lot more effect on your score.

The confidence that comes from knowledge and practice creates its own energy. If you are confident and get good results, you become a little more confident and achieve better results. Remember that confidence feeds off itself.

> The confidence
>
> that comes from
>
> knowledge and
>
> practice creates
>
> its own energy.

In closing, here is an anecdote about keeping cool. A friend of mine, Bob Forte, caddied for Willie Turnesa, who was one of the great amateur players of the 1940s and '50s. Mr. Turnesa was the most accomplished amateur player since Bobby Jones. Among his many career highlights, Willie "The Wedge" Turnesa won one British and two U.S. Amateurs and played on three Walker Cup Teams.

Willie Turnesa was seventy-five years old when my friend caddied for him at Ridgewood Country Club. Willie had a score of 70. Bob asked him for some golf advice and was somewhat disappointed when Willie Turnesa told him to keep his head still. My friend looked at him curiously, with an "is that all there is" type of look. With a twinkle in his eye, Mr. Turnesa pointed his index finger to his temple and said, "You have to keep your 'head' still."

Please absorb the information in this book, practice, stay cool, and enjoy this wonderful game.

Glossary

Addressing the ball: Taking a stance by placing the feet in position for making a stroke and by grounding the club. In a bunker, taking a stance in preparation for making a stroke.

Approach: A stroke or shot to the putting green.

Backspin: Backward rotation of the ball, causing it to stop abruptly.

Backswing: Bringing the club up behind the body in preparation for the stroke.

Bounce (of the sand wedge): The extra metal on the back of the sand wedge that prevents the clubhead from digging into the sand and allows it to glide through the sand instead.

Break: In putting, to play to either side of the direct line from the ball to the hole to compensate for any roll or slant in the green.

Bunker: An area of bare ground, often a marked depression, usually covered with sand.

Chip: A short approach shot in which the ball flies close to the ground and then rolls.

Claw grip: Putting grip in which the top hand holds the putter in its normal grip, then the bottom hand is placed on the handle so that the handle rests between the thumb and middle finger. The four fingers of the bottom hand rest on the top of the handle. All four knuckles of the bottom hand are visible, and it looks more like a claw than a hand.

Cross-handed grip: Grip in which the hands are reversed from their standard grip.

Downswing: The downward stroke of the club, from behind the body to the ball.

Equator: Middle of the ball.

Face: The part of the clubhead that strikes the ball.

Fairway: The closely cut grass intended for play between the tee and the green.

Flop shot: A pitch shot in which the ball makes a high, lofted arc and a soft landing with little roll. Also known as a lob shot.

Follow-through: Continuation of the swing of the club after the ball has been struck.

Gap wedge: Club that has a loft angle of between 46 and 56 degrees.

Green: The putting green or very closely mown area around the cup.

Lie: The inclination of the club when held on the ground in the natural position for striking; also, the position of the ball on the ground.

Line: The direct path between the ball and the hold.

Lob: Approach shot in which the ball has a high arc and a soft landing. Also known as a flop shot.

Lob wedge: Club that has a loft angle of between 58 and 68 degrees.

Loft: Angle between the clubface and the ground.

Long putter: Putter designed with an extra-long handle; the handle is anchored against the chest during the putt to stabilize the putter.

Pitch: An approach shot in which the ball flies onto the green, either in a high, lofted arc or a low, running shot.

Pitching wedge: Club that has a loft angle of between 42 to 49 degrees and a bounce of between 0 and 10 degrees.

Putt: A stroke made on a putting green in which the ball stays on the ground.

Putting green: The ground around the hole that is specifically prepared for putting. Also known as the green.

Rough: Long grass bordering the fairway, which may include bushes and trees.

Run: To hit the ball along the ground in an approach instead of chipping or pitching it; also, the distance a ball rolls after it lands.

Sand wedge: Club that has a loft angle of between 54 and 56 degrees and a bounce, or extra weight on the bottom of the clubhead, to help it glide through the sand.

Stance: The position of the feet and body when a player is addressing the ball.

Stroke: The forward movement of the club with the intention of striking the ball.

Sweet spot: The middle of the clubface, considered the best spot to hit the ball.

Ten-finger grip: Grip in which both hands hold the handle of the club, with no interlocking or overlapping of the fingers.

Wrist hinge or break: Movement of the wrist during the stroke.

Yips: A severe putting disorder characterized by muscle spasms in the arms.

Index